SPEECHLESS

Nevertheless, Thy Will Be Done.

"Father, if you are willing, take this cup from me; yet not my will, but yours be done."
Luke 22:46

stephanie d. moore
Edited by
Debra M. Smith

Published by
Moore Marketing and Communications, LLC

Oklahoma City, OK
StephanieDMoore.com
MooretoRead.com

Bulk copies or group sales of this book are available by contacting Stephanie D. Moore at moore@stephaniedmoore.com or (405) 306-9833.

Moore, Stephanie D.
Speechless: Nevertheless, Thy Will Be Done.
A 31-Day Devotional

Edited by Debra M. Smith

First Edition Printed June 2023
Printed in the USA.

Cover Design and Layout Design by
Moore Marketing and Communications, LLC.

Cover Photo used in design retrieved at pexels.com, taken by Rebound Cities.

ISBN:978-1-955544-44-3

"Father, if you are willing, take this cup from me;
yet not my will, but yours be done."

Luke 22:42

SPEECHLESS

Nevertheless, Thy Will Be Done.

In Loving Memory

Michael & Brenda Bradley

But he said to me, "My grace is sufficient for you, for my power is made perfect in weakness." Therefore I will boast all the more gladly about my weaknesses, so that Christ's power may rest on me.

2 Corinthians 12:9

To Die is Gain

Let us not love with words or speech but with actions and in truth.
1 John 3:18

Everything we say has power. Words are containers of power that echo over time. Once we speak, our words have the potential to reach many destinations and the ability to generate unexpected and unintended outcomes.

I am certain we can all remember the most hateful words spoken to us. At least, in that moment, even if it hurt, we knew how the person felt about us and that they were being honest. What about the first time we told someone that we loved them and they responded in kind? Our hearts and minds were filled with a joy that cannot be adequately expressed by words, but simply by the way it made us feel. Perhaps we can consider the moment when a negotiated trust was formed; an agreement that defined a beginning, a purpose, and an intended destination. It was a promise that created an expectation.

But words without actions that mirror the sentiment are simply words. They symbolically march into the room decorated with pomp and circumstance, dancing in the minds of the receiver until what should happen does not. They echo in our minds becoming tares among the wheat, pretending to be what they are not. Then a bitter root of resentment, distrust, and disappointment resonates and results in a separation between the speaker of words and the expected recipient of actions not taken.

Our commitment to do what we say is coupled with our integrity, holiness, and representation as an ambassador of Christ.

God does not hold us to a standard that he himself is not willing to uphold. The grace of God extends to each of us. We do not deserve it, yet we receive it. Likewise, we are not called to be perfect, but when we accept Christ as our Lord and Savior, he calls us to be holy.

Holiness is not perfection, yet it distinctly refuses to accept sin as a lifestyle. It does not praise Jesus and cuss out our neighbor. It does not steal, kill, and destroy every day to get ahead. Instead, holiness allows our words and our actions to align in parallel fashion, walking hand-in-hand that Christ may abound in our hearts, minds, actions and environments. Holiness is pervasive, it leaves no stone unturned. It impacts every aspect of our lives.

So what? Are we to be holier than thou robots, judging others, beating them with scripture and pointing out their mistakes? No. That is not what it means. It means that we must learn that we are human and that others are human as well. No one is perfect, but we can be holy. This is why we must let love and forgiveness reign in our hearts.

We reflect our love for others by being good to them - especially when they need it most. Our most difficult communications are to be presented with love and seasoned with grace. We extend mercy when others disappoint us, we give without the expectation of receiving, we continue to protect those who do not appreciate our protection, and we forgive those who hurt us. Our goal is to become a perfect conduit of God's message and love, creating a path for the Lord to travel.

To die is gain. Jesus Christ is our example. He died that we may live. He endured the ridicule of the cross, the pain of betrayal, and the rejection of his love for us.

By the power of the Holy Spirit, we embody a 'nevertheless, thy will be done' lifestyle.

Prayer

Most Gracious and Heavenly Father,

Thank you for your unconditional love, mercy, and grace. May the words of our mouths and the meditations of our hearts be pleasing in your sight, Lord, our Rock and our Redeemer. [1] *For all things are permissible but not everything is beneficial. Everything is permissible but not everything is edifying.* [2] *Therefore, seeing we also are surrounded by a great cloud of witnesses, let us lay aside every weight, and the sin which so easily besets us, and let us run with patience the race that is set before us, looking unto Jesus, the author and finisher of our faith, who for the joy that was set before Him endured the cross, despising the shame, and is set down at the right hand of the throne of God.* [3]

And whatever we do, whether in word or deed, may we do it all in the name of the Lord Jesus, giving thanks to God the Father through him. [4]

In Jesus Name,

Amen

God's Will Be Done

He asked me, "Son of man, can these bones live?"
I said, "Sovereign Lord, you alone know."
Ezekiel 37:3

When all is lost and our hope has been depleted, we turn to God with questions and on our worst days, doubt. We wonder if our living has been in vain and whether God knows about our situation.

He knows. He cares. He lives.

When I have a large project in front of me, it helps me to visualize each area and the activities required for all the moving parts to join and become one. I imagine all of the stakeholders, those with ownership, and specific outcomes I hope to generate. I try to imagine each person's experience, how they will feel and perhaps even respond.

When God took Ezekiel to the valley of dry bones, he had a clear purpose. He wanted Ezekiel to gain clarity around three principals - visualization, prophecy, and God's omnipotent sovereignty.

When we walk through our own personal valleys of dry bones - debt, domestic violence, addiction, depression, death, and caregiver stress - we must look to Jesus, the author and finisher of our faith.

Facing Reality

As God demonstrated for Ezekiel in chapter 37, we

must first see our situation as it is (a valley of dry bones). God led Ezekiel back and forth in the valley so that he fully understood the breadth of the situation. Only with clarity and understanding can we move forward to solution-based thinking.

We Must Turn to God & Prophesy

As Ezekiel walked through the valley, God asked him if the situation could change. Ezekiel admitted that there was no way for him to know, that only God knew. In response, God told Ezekiel to prophesy and to say exactly what he said. Ezekiel had to prophesy twice for things to happen. As he spoke, he believed. As he believed, he witnessed a change.

Sovereign God

At the end of the day, all that we experience is to shine a light on the love of God that he may win souls to Christ. The lesson in the valley of dry bones was to reveal to Ezekiel that God was going to join the body of Christ, two split factions (at the time represented by Judah and Israel) together as one that they could worship him together in Zion. When we recognize that God is in control, that he sees our suffering and understands even the most minute details of our lives, we learn to trust him. Then we will experience the blessings of Zion - peace, love, and abundance in unity with God.

Facing our reality may not be difficult because at times our reality can be loud and demanding, insisting we pay attention and pay attention now. It can be overwhelming and feel like a never-ending burden. We are not alone. God is with us, and he understands. He wants to carry our burdens. He wants to heal our land. He wants to restore us to a place of peace, joy, and happiness. But we must truly inspect our situation, bring it to him, and do what he says to do. He alone can identify the source of our issue and give us the words that will bring life. We must do as he says, and like Ezekiel, we must do it until we see a change.

By the power of the Holy Spirit, we embody a 'nevertheless, thy will be done' lifestyle.

Prayer

Most Gracious and Heavenly Father,

Thank you for your unconditional love, mercy, and grace. May the words of our mouths and the meditations of our hearts be pleasing in your sight, Lord, our Rock and our Redeemer. [(1)] *For all things are permissible but not everything is beneficial. Everything is permissible but not everything is edifying.* [(2)] *Therefore, seeing we also are surrounded by a great cloud of witnesses, let us lay aside every weight, and the sin which so easily besets us, and let us run with patience the race that is set before us, looking unto Jesus, the author and finisher of our faith, who for the joy that was set before Him endured the cross, despising the shame, and is set down at the right hand of the throne of God.* [(3)]

We prophesy and say: 'This is what the Sovereign Lord says: My people, I am going to open your graves and bring you up from them; I will bring you back to the land of Israel. Then you, my people, will know that I am the Lord, when I open your graves and bring you up from them. I will put my Spirit in you, and you will live, and I will settle you in your own land. Then you will know that I the Lord have spoken, and I have done it, declares the Lord.' [(5)]

In Jesus' Name,

Amen

Bless Them Anyway

But the Lord replied, "Is it right for you to be angry?"
Jonah 4:4

Recently, I was tasked with hosting an event and working with a fairly new group of people under my direction. I have a type A personality and as a black woman, that does not always jive well with a group of predominantly white males who also happen to be type A. But honestly, the males would always listen to reason, (as my anger at moments was not wholly unfounded) but it was the white woman in the group that never relented in her disrespectful disposition (right or wrong).

This all happened at a time when I was being paid for 25 hours a week, but working 80. When I complained about it, the client simply told me to "deal with it." He thought my 80 was more like 30. This too angered me.

I was overworked, disrespected, and underpaid. Perhaps it would be different if everything I made wasn't going right back out the door... every dollar I made was going toward insurance, rent, and family. I had nothing to look forward to and life felt dark, lonely, and hopeless.

So when God began to bless this group through the company I served, my anger reached an all-time high. I could relate to Jonah and his distaste for God's mercy on Nineveh.

The question in our key scripture that God asked Jonah is the same question God asked me. You see, there were many times and will be many times when I will need the mercy of

God to see me through and God is no respecter of persons. He doesn't honor one of us or any of us over another. We all will have our moments in the sun.

While I am still a little hurt about what has transpired, I know God is right in his decision making and I thank God that he is driving. While it doesn't change my current state of pain with this client, or lessen the weight of my overbearing financial situation, it does help to soften my anger. I know I have benefitted from the mercy of God, and we should all appreciate it when we not only experience it but can bear witness to it.

We cannot curse what God has decided to bless, and at times, he will use us to bless those who we may deem less likely to deserve it.

By the power of the Holy Spirit, we embody a 'nevertheless, thy will be done' lifestyle.

Prayer

Most Gracious and Heavenly Father,

Thank you for your unconditional love, mercy, and grace. May the words of our mouths and the meditations of our hearts be pleasing in your sight, Lord, our Rock and our Redeemer. [1] *For all things are permissible but not everything is beneficial. Everything is permissible but not everything is edifying.* [2] *Therefore, seeing we also are surrounded by a great cloud of witnesses, let us lay aside every weight, and the sin which so easily besets us, and let us run with patience the race that is set before us, looking unto Jesus, the author and finisher of our faith, who for the joy that was set before Him endured the cross, despising the shame, and is set down at the right hand of the throne of God.* [3]

In our distress we called to the Lord, and he answered us. From deep in the realm of the dead we called for help, and he listened to our cry. The Lord hurled us into the depths, into the very heart of the seas, and the currents swirled about us; all the waves and breakers swept over us. We said, 'We have been banished from your sight; yet we will look again toward your holy temple.' The engulfing waters threatened us, the deep surrounded us; seaweed was wrapped around our heads. To the roots of the mountains we sank down; the earth beneath barred us in forever. But you, Lord our God, brought our lives up from the pit. When our lives were ebbing away, we remembered you, Lord, and our prayers rose to you, to your holy temple. Those who cling to worthless idols turn away from God's love for them. But I, with shouts of grateful praise, will sacrifice to you. What I have vowed I will make good. I will say, 'Salvation comes from the Lord. (6)

In Jesus' Name,

Amen

It's Not About Us

Because Joseph her husband was faithful to the law, and yet did not want to expose her to public disgrace, he had in mind to divorce her quietly.

But after he had considered this, an angel of the Lord appeared to him in a dream and said, "Joseph son of David, do not be afraid to take Mary home as your wife, because what is conceived in her is from the Holy Spirit. She will give birth to a son, and you are to give him the name Jesus, because he will save his people from their sins."

Matthew 1:19-20

Every now and again God will position us to bless others at our great expense. It can be uncomfortable and undesirable, but when we recognize in our hearts that God is telling us to do something, we must.

Mary and Joseph were in love. They were young, faithful to God, and believed their life had a very promising future. At that time, as it is in ideal situations today, the young maiden Mary was a virgin. She'd saved herself for marriage and Joseph was proud to have her on his arm. They were a young and equally yoked couple that were positioned to succeed and probably expected to live society's definition of a good life (a nice home, beautiful family, thriving careers, and openly committed to their faith). Everyone knew of their commitment to one another and was aware of their engagement.

One evening, Mary was visited by an angel who informed her that she would carry the Messiah. She did not question it and accepted what the angel shared. After Mary informed Joseph she was pregnant by the Holy Spirit, he decided to annul his commitment to her and quietly move on. But before he was able to take any action, he too was visited by an angel that insisted Joseph marry her and raise the child as his son. Joseph also accepted what the angel instructed.

Joseph and Mary endured difficult assignments. The assignments they were given changed the trajectory of their lives forever. While they still went on to marry and have other children, the purity of what they once shared was never the same. Yet their love for God never changed and they filled the assignment which has blessed us all.

By the power of the Holy Spirit, we embody a 'nevertheless, thy will be done' lifestyle.

Prayer

Most Gracious and Heavenly Father,

Thank you for your unconditional love, mercy, and grace. May the words of our mouths and the meditations of our hearts be pleasing in your sight, Lord, our Rock and our Redeemer. [(1)] *For all things are permissible but not everything is beneficial. Everything is permissible but not everything is edifying.* [(2)] *Therefore, seeing we also are surrounded by a great cloud of witnesses, let us lay aside every weight, and the sin which so easily besets us, and let us run with patience the race that is set before us, looking unto Jesus, the author and finisher of our faith, who for the joy that was set before Him endured the cross, despising the shame, and is set down at the right hand of the throne of God.* [(3)]

Blessed are those who trust in the Lord, who do not look to the proud, to those who turn aside to false gods. Many, Lord our God, are the wonders you have done, the things you planned for us. None can compare with you; were we to speak and tell of your deeds, they would be too many to declare. Sacrifice and offering you did not desire—but our ears you have opened—burnt offerings and sin offerings you did not require. Then we said, "Here we are, we have come—it is written about us in the scroll. We desire to do your will, our God; your law is within our hearts." (7)

In Jesus' Name,

Amen

Life for Life

So the men answered her, "Our lives for yours, if none of you tell this business of ours. And it shall be, when the Lord has given us the land, that we will deal kindly and truly with you."

Joshua 2:14

When our back is against the wall and we are all alone, we raise our fists up in protection, we ready our minds to be full of determination even while shrouded by fear, and our heart carefully measures every rhythm to ensure we are surviving what is before us heartbeat by heartbeat. We instinctively recognize that our next decision could be our last, greatly impacting our lives and more importantly, the lives of those we love.

Every person living has faced a "fork in the road" decision. Some faced it behind the wheel of a car, others while looking down the barrel of a gun, and even others while deciding whether to cheat, lie, or steal to gain access to resources seemingly out of reach. God teaches us to always choose life that it may be well with us and our children.

Our faith is often tested as we decide whether we will abide by heavenly will or earthly authority, but we cannot choose both. We are tasked with not only recognizing God's sovereignty but are called to trust in his ability to protect us. God asks us to jeopardize what we recognize as life and safety to gain true life and eternal peace.

Joshua was a new leader of Israel (after Moses) and was told by God to send spies to search the land, but especially the land of Jericho. When the men Joshua sent arrived in Jericho, they stopped at the house of a local prostitute named Rahab. The king got word that the spies were in her home and that they had come to search the entire country. So the king sent his servants to retrieve the men of God.

As the men approached her home, Rahab hid the men of God on the rooftop, under the sheaves to conceal their presence. When the king's men arrived and inquired of the men, Rahab lied to them and told them that while they did stay with her, she did not know where the men were from but that they had narrowly escaped before the city gates shut for the evening. But she told them that if they hurried, they would probably be able to catch the men. Once the men were gone, she went to the men of God and asked them for a favor.

Rahab recognized the men as Israelites and told them that everyone in her community was in a state of dread because of their presence. The local men heard the stories of God rescuing them from Pharaoh in Egypt and how their enemies had drowned in the Red Sea, after God opened the sea and allowed them to pass over safely. The people of Jericho knew the Israelites were protected by God.

While there is no indication that Rahab had a personal relationship with God, she recognized his sovereignty. Rahab had never met God or any people of God to know that they would deal righteously with her, yet she chose to honor God anyway. When her back was against the wall and it was time to make a critical decision, she chose to trust God who saved the Israelite slaves from oppression and destroyed their enemy. In return, she simply asked for the Israelite men to protect she and her family when the time came for them to seize the land of Jericho. The men promised her that they would, but her continued obedience would be necessary for it to happen.

God will ask us to choose his will and his way over what to others may seem like the right choice or answer. As we choose God, we will be challenged. So much so that our deliverance and protection will require our continued obedience. Yet when we sacrifice our lives for the life God has called us to live, we gain eternal love, joy, peace, provision, and protection.

By the power of the Holy Spirit, we embody a 'nevertheless, thy will be done' lifestyle.

Prayer

Most Gracious and Heavenly Father,

Thank you for your unconditional love, mercy, and grace. May the words of our mouths and the meditations of our hearts be pleasing in your sight, Lord, our Rock and our Redeemer. [(1)] *For all things are permissible but not everything is beneficial. Everything is permissible but not everything is edifying.* [(2)] *Therefore, seeing we also are surrounded by a great cloud of witnesses, let us lay aside every weight, and the sin which so easily besets us, and let us run with patience the race that is set before us, looking unto Jesus, the author and finisher of our faith, who for the joy that was set before Him endured the cross, despising the shame, and is set down at the right hand of the throne of God.* [(3)]

We will lift up our eyes to the mountains— where does our help come from? Our help comes from the Lord, the Maker of heaven and earth. He will not let our foot slip—he who watches over us will not slumber; indeed, he who watches over Israel will neither slumber nor sleep. The Lord watches over us—the Lord is our shade at our right hand; the sun will not harm us by day, nor the moon by night. The Lord will keep us from all harm—he will watch over our lives; the Lord will watch over our coming and going both now and forevermore. (8)

In Jesus' Name,

Amen

One Fold, One Shepherd

My sheep hear my voice, and I know them, and they follow me.

John 10:27

Sin is pervasive and subtle; it pulls those who are most dedicated away at times. But God, who is our Good Shepherd, will never leave us nor forsake us, he risked his life for ours.

I wish to God I was a perfect person. I wish I could say I never sin but I do. I try to live a life that is holy and honors God, but I fall short, daily. At moments, anger and indignation, at others, pride, selfishness and greed. Even when we spend time with God and decide in our hearts that we are going to go "hard for Christ" we fail.

Jesus told Peter that he would betray him three times before the cock crowed, but Peter wouldn't believe it - until it happened. We can live our lives doing our best to honor God and fail. But it doesn't mean we shouldn't try and keep trying after we fall.

God loves us. He knows us. This is why he laid down his life for us. We were born in sin. But sin's only desire is to kill, steal and destroy us. This is something we must remember as we make decisions. While God will always forgive us, protect us, and provide for us - sin's desire is to destroy all the good that God has created in our lives. We must choose life that it can be good for us and for those we love.

We can only be persuaded to choose life if we are open to hearing God's voice. When we hear God speaking to us, we recognize it. We cannot turn a blind eye to God and say, "I will return once my sinning is complete." Sin separates us from

God. It keeps us from seeking his face and causes us to seek his hand. God cannot bless our mess.

It is not in our power to always say no to the sin which so easily besets us. But with the help of the Holy Spirit, we can. By the power of the Holy Spirit, we embody a 'nevertheless, thy will be done' lifestyle.

Prayer

Most Gracious and Heavenly Father,

Thank you for your unconditional love, mercy, and grace. May the words of our mouths and the meditations of our hearts be pleasing in your sight, Lord, our Rock and our Redeemer. [(1)] *For all things are permissible but not everything is beneficial. Everything is permissible but not everything is edifying.* [(2)] *Therefore, seeing we also are surrounded by a great cloud of witnesses, let us lay aside every weight, and the sin which so easily besets us, and let us run with patience the race that is set before us, looking unto Jesus, the author and finisher of our faith, who for the joy that was set before Him endured the cross, despising the shame, and is set down at the right hand of the throne of God.* [(3)]

The law of the Lord is perfect, reviving the soul; the testimony of the Lord is sure, making wise the simple; the precepts of the Lord are right, rejoicing the heart; the commandment of the Lord is pure, enlightening the eyes; the fear of the Lord is clean, enduring forever; the rules of the Lord are true, and righteous altogether. More to be desired are they than gold, even much fine gold; sweeter also than honey and drippings of the honeycomb. Moreover, by them are your servants warned; in keeping them there is great reward. Who can discern his errors? Declare us innocent from hidden faults. Keep back your servants also from presumptuous sins; let them not have dominion over us! Then we shall be blameless, and innocent of great transgression. Let the words of our mouths and the meditation of our hearts be acceptable in your sight, O Lord, our rock and our redeemer. (9)

In Jesus' Name,

Amen

Perseverance to Preach

When he would not be dissuaded, we gave up and said, "The Lord's will be done."

Acts 21:14

When God asks us to do his will, he has already gone before us to make every crooked place straight. He knows every oppositional threat and every devious deed done in the dark. He knows who will grant us favor and has softened the hearts of those we need to accomplish his will.

Paul, once named Saul, was converted to Christianity as he traveled to persecute those who believed in Jesus Christ. After Saul met Jesus, he was named Paul and began to preach the gospel wherever he went. As a Jew, his testimony was not received by his fellow Jews, so Paul preached to the Gentiles, which angered the Jewish leadership even more.

After a while on the road, preaching to the Gentiles, he realized the will of God was for him to return to Jerusalem, where he would preach the gospel to the Jews. The other disciples pleaded for him not to return as they thought the Jews would plot to kill him.

Upon his arrival in Jerusalem, Paul initially attempted to disguise himself, while also attempting to outwardly reflect one who had cleansed himself of all iniquity to the Jews. But once he was recognized in a temple, he was taken and almost beaten to death. The Roman soldiers broke up the commotion and took him captive.

Paul was on trial before the Jews defending the gospel

of Jesus Christ. The Roman soldiers did not understand the charges against him, and once they found out he was a Roman citizen by birth did not feel comfortable participating in any of the trials. When they discovered that a plot was underway to take Paul's life, they wanted to wash their hands of it, and sent him from Jerusalem to Caesarea to be tried. The Roman governor, Felix, sent for the Jews that accused him to stand trial. At the end of yet another trial, the Roman king did not see fit to sentence Paul to death, and instead held him in prison until the end of his political term. At the end of the term, he kept Paul in prison as political leadership transferred to another, Festus.

All the while, Paul was forced to recant his defense and share the gospel with many including King Agrippa. King Agrippa came to hear Paul's defense because the Jews asked the new governor, Festus to transfer him back to Jerusalem where they planned to kill him. But Paul prevented it by appealing to Caesar which was his right as a Roman citizen. King Agrippa came to help Festus determine the charges that should be sent to Caesar with Paul when he was transferred. King Agrippa decided that Paul should be released but because he appealed to Caesar he must go forward.

When Paul was sent to Rome to stand trial before Caesar, he went by ship which encountered a hurricane and left them stranded on an island for three months. During that time, he preached the gospel, healed the sick and was able to live under a single guard. When he finally arrived in Rome three months later, he was allowed to rent a home, preach the gospel to anyone who stopped by, and live at peace.

Every moment of doing God's will requires courage, strength, and faith. God is in control. He knows the end from the beginning and does not seek to see us fail.

By the power of the Holy Spirit, we embody a 'nevertheless, thy will be done' lifestyle.

Prayer

Most Gracious and Heavenly Father,

Thank you for your unconditional love, mercy, and grace. May the words of our mouths and the meditations of our hearts be pleasing in your sight, Lord, our Rock and our Redeemer. [(1)] *For all things are permissible but not everything is beneficial. Everything is permissible but not everything is edifying.* [(2)] *Therefore, seeing we also are surrounded by a great cloud of witnesses, let us lay aside every weight, and the sin which so easily besets us, and let us run with patience the race that is set before us, looking unto Jesus, the author and finisher of our faith, who for the joy that was set before Him endured the cross, despising the shame, and is set down at the right hand of the throne of God.* [(3)]

If the Lord had not been on our side—let Israel say—if the Lord had not been on our side when people attacked us, they would have swallowed us alive when their anger flared against us; the flood would have engulfed us, the torrent would have swept over us, the raging waters would have swept us away. Praise be to the Lord, who has not let us be torn by their teeth. We have escaped like a bird from the fowler's snare; the snare has been broken, and we have escaped. Our help is in the name of the Lord, the Maker of heaven and earth. (10)

In Jesus' Name,

Amen

Called by God

"Pardon me, my lord," Gideon replied, "but how can I save Israel? My clan is the weakest in Manasseh, and I am the least in my family."

The Lord answered, "I will be with you, and you will strike down all the Midianites, leaving none alive."

Judges 6:15-16

At times, we may see ourselves or the work we do as insignificant. We may believe that we are not important or that what we do is not important, but this is a plot of the evil one to diminish our value. If we give up on believing that we are a critical component to the big picture, the enemy can get a toe in and destroy what God has created.

Gideon was a man in the Bible that was doing what was necessary for his family to survive. They were an oppressed people fighting to secure their future and provide for their families. But because of the great adversity they faced with the people of the land, they were hiding and doing what they did secretly to avoid their profits being stolen.

An angel of the Lord approached Gideon and asked him to do something great for God that would bless his people.

But Gideon found it hard to believe that God would use him for such an amazing feat. He asked God to verify it was really him asking Gideon for these things and that it was not simply Gideon's imagination running wild.

God did it. He proved (in many ways) to Gideon that he wasn't imagining things, that God was really speaking directly to him, and that God had prepared him to do great things.

Gideon began to trust God's voice and he obeyed God. By the power of the Holy Spirit, we embody a 'nevertheless, thy will be done' lifestyle.

Prayer

Most Gracious and Heavenly Father,

Thank you for your unconditional love, mercy, and grace. May the words of our mouths and the meditations of our hearts be pleasing in your sight, Lord, our Rock and our Redeemer. [(1)] *For all things are permissible but not everything is beneficial. Everything is permissible but not everything is edifying.* [(2)] *Therefore, seeing we also are surrounded by a great cloud of witnesses, let us lay aside every weight, and the sin which so easily besets us, and let us run with patience the race that is set before us, looking unto Jesus, the author and finisher of our faith, who for the joy that was set before Him endured the cross, despising the shame, and is set down at the right hand of the throne of God.* [(3)]

You have searched us, Lord, and you know us. You know when we sit and when we rise; you perceive our thoughts from afar. You discern our going out and our lying down; you are familiar with all our ways. Before a word is on our tongues you, Lord, know it completely. You hem us in behind and before, and you lay your hand upon us. Such knowledge is too wonderful for us, too lofty to attain. Where can we go from your Spirit? Where can we flee from your presence? If we go up to the heavens, you are there; if we make our beds in the depths, you are there. If we rise on the wings of the dawn, if we settle on the far side of the sea, even there your hand will guide us, your right hand will hold us fast. If we say, "Surely the darkness will hide us and the light become night around us," even the darkness will not be dark to you; the night will shine like the day, for darkness is as light to you. For you created our inmost being, you knit us together in our mother's womb. We praise you because we are fearfully and wonderfully made; your works are wonderful; we know that full well. Our frame was not hidden from you when we were made in the secret place, when we were woven together in the depths of the earth. Your eyes saw our unformed body; all the days ordained for each of us were written in your book before one of them came to be. How precious to us are your thoughts, God! How vast is the sum of them! Were we to count them, they would outnumber the grains of sand—when we awake, we are still with you. If only you, God, would slay the wicked! Away from us, you who are bloodthirsty! They speak of you with evil intent; your adversaries misuse your name. Do we not hate those who hate you, Lord, and abhor those who are in rebellion against you? We have nothing but hatred for them; we count them our enemies. Search us, God, and know our hearts; test us and know our anxious thoughts. See if there is any offensive way in us, and lead us in the way everlasting. (11)

In Jesus' Name,

Amen

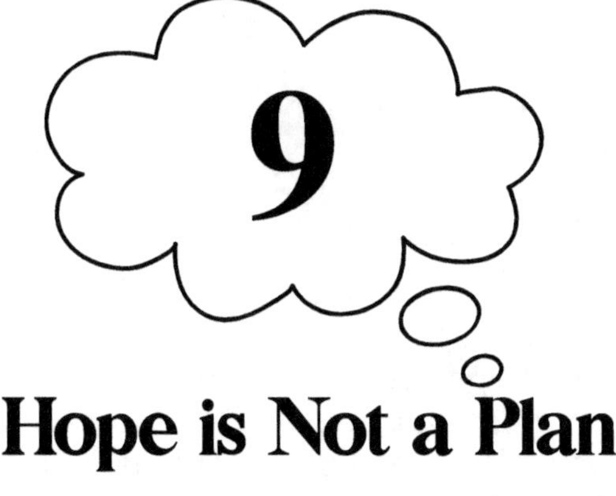

Hope is Not a Plan

But Saul and the army spared Agag and the best of the sheep and cattle, the fat calves and lambs—everything that was good. These they were unwilling to destroy completely, but everything that was despised and weak they totally destroyed.

I Samuel 15:9

Recipes provide clear instructions that will result in an expected outcome. In a similar way, God has a desire for each of us to reach an expected destination, but our journeys are defined by our unique DNA, our environment and his guidance.

Just as the necessary ingredients of any recipe contain specific amounts of natural substance which when combined with an explicit method of cooking create our desired dish, our journeys must also possess the particular details required to reach God's intended destination. Every step must be taken in order and executed with precision to reach that end. But when we substitute our way for God's way, unexpected outcomes occur and unfortunately, we and those we love most, may be at the receiving end of the negativity that results.

Saul was anointed by God to be king. But he lacked patience and good judgment. God wanted to avenge the treatment of the Israelites as they journeyed from Egypt by the Amalekites who refused to offer them safe passage. He clearly instructed Saul to destroy every person and animal. But instead, Saul did it his way. He and his men kept what was "good" in their sight, as opposed to following God's clear instruction. As a result, his ability to remain king was stripped from he and his lineage and handed over to a man after God's own heart, David.

When Samuel the prophet was told by God all that Saul had done, Samuel cried all night. In the morning, he went to visit the king. King Saul stood proudly and smiled at his "obedience" to God, rendering only a portion of what God instructed, not all. He hoped that his plan was good enough to please God because it pleased him. But God viewed his disobedience as Saul turning away from God.

Samuel the prophet was angry. He informed Saul of what God said. God had given Saul the kingdom but with such honor came great responsibility. His responsibility was to obey God. Saul insisted he did obey God. But in doing so, he interpreted that he had the freedom to change or add to what God instructed and tried to outwit Samuel and God by using the exact terminology of God and the unsanctioned worship of God to justify his actions.

Samuel clearly defined something for Saul that we must all adopt and understand.

"To obey is better than sacrifice, and to heed is better than the fat of rams. For rebellion is like the sin of divination, and arrogance like the evil of idolatry." (12)

Saul immediately repented but it was too late. His leadership had been stripped from he and his bloodline and given to another. Samuel immediately finished the work that God assigned Saul to do; he killed the King of the Amalekites.

The irony in the situation is that Saul determined what was worthy of keeping, based on what was deemed the "best" quality. In doing so, he immediately marked himself as "despised and weak" in God's eyes. This rendered the irony that God also opted to select what was good and best and to completely destroy what was "despised and weak" in his eyes - a disobedient king.

Saul never recovered from his sin and was subsequently taunted by evil spirits until the day he died while hunting for David, who was anointed to be the next king and ordained to carry the lineage of Jesus Christ.

Obedience often requires us to do what is difficult. Much like our favorite recipe, if we follow the clear instructions as provided without wavering, we can reap what we expect. It is when we substitute, add, or subtract that unexpected results are rendered. By the power of the Holy Spirit, we embody a 'nevertheless, thy will be done' lifestyle.

Prayer

Thank you for your unconditional love, mercy, and grace. May the words of our mouths and the meditations of our hearts be pleasing in your sight, Lord, our Rock and our Redeemer. [(1)] *For all things are permissible but not everything is beneficial. Everything is permissible but not everything is edifying.* [(2)] *Therefore, seeing we also are surrounded by a great cloud of witnesses, let us lay aside every weight, and the sin which so easily besets us, and let us run with patience the race that is set before us, looking unto Jesus, the author and finisher of our faith, who for the joy that was set before Him endured the cross, despising the shame, and is set down at the right hand of the throne of God.* [(3)]

Sacrifice and offering you do not desire—but our ears you have opened—burnt offerings and sin offerings you do not require. We say, "Here we are, we have come—it is written about us in the scroll. We desire to do your will, our God; your law is within our hearts." We proclaim your saving acts in the great assembly; we do not seal our lips, Lord, as you know. We do not hide your righteousness in our hearts; we speak of your faithfulness and your saving help. We do not conceal your love and your faithfulness from the great assembly. Do not withhold your mercy from us, Lord; may your love and faithfulness always protect us. For troubles without number surround us; our sins have overtaken us, and we cannot see. They are more than the hairs of our head, and our heart fails within us. Be pleased to save us, Lord; come quickly, Lord, to help us. May all who want to take our lives be put to shame and confusion; may all who desire our ruin be turned back in disgrace. May those who say to us, "Aha! Aha!" be appalled at their own shame. But may all who seek you rejoice and be glad in you; may those who long for your saving help always say, "The Lord is great!" But as for us, we are poor and needy; may the Lord think of us. You are our help and our deliverer; you are our God, do not delay. (13)

In Jesus' Name,

Amen

Sovereign Over All

So the governors and satraps sought to find some charge against Daniel concerning the kingdom; but they could find no charge or fault, because he was faithful; nor was there any error or fault found in him. Then these men said, "We shall not find any charge against this Daniel unless we find it against him concerning the law of his God."

Daniel 6:4-5

Communications are at the core of understanding the needs of those we serve, whether it be family, friends, an employer, or a community member in distress. Communications are also pivotal to sharing perspective, creating plans, and the submission of information. God expects us to communicate with him at all times (sending and receiving his messages), as the Bible shares for us to pray without ceasing. In doing so, we are not only communicating with God, but we are also providing recognition to not only his authority in our lives, but his sovereignty over all.

One of my clients has issued a company credit card in my name to be used when necessary. I often use the card multiple times per week for various incidentals, including lunch with stakeholders. As I have been with the company for less than three years, I find it critically important that all these incidentals are communicated, well documented and approved prior to use. After use, I submit my documentation of receipts and actual use to the accounting department in a timely manner. I also work lock and step with a videographer who documents a lot of the work that we do in the community for the sake of public relations. Each time

I schedule his services, he confirms with me the intended purpose and desired shots to be captured. If we interview anyone on site, he asks if there are specific viewpoints I would like the person being interviewed to share. Petitions are at the center of workflow and guided direction ensures that there is no gap in coverage.

Daniel was a Hebrew boy that was held captive in Babylon. However, because Daniel proved to be very intelligent and wise, he was elevated to a leadership position. He was one of three leaders that led a team of one hundred and twenty and was found to be an efficient, hard worker. Those he worked with knew Daniel would pray to God throughout the day (as Daniel did this in a publicized manner where he could be witnessed as one who honored his culture).

The other leaders were jealous of Daniel and devised a plot to destroy him. So a group of the leaders and the one hundred and twenty they led went to the king and asked,

"King Darius, live forever! All the governors of the kingdom, the administrators and satraps, the counselors and advisors, have consulted together to establish a royal statute and to make a firm decree, that whoever petitions any god or man for thirty days, except you, O king, shall be cast into the den of lions. Now, O king, establish the decree and sign the writing, so that it cannot be changed, according to the law of the Medes and Persians, which does not alter." (14)

So, in essence, they restricted all manner of structural communication in the kingdom for thirty days, making it illegal for any man to ask for anything from a man or spiritual deity except the king. Daniel realized that his activity as a supervisor and more importantly, his worship was at the center of their targeted request to the king.

Unfortunately for them, Daniel knew who was sovereign and he was forced to reflect the ultimate authority he honored in his life. His actions were not in disrespect to the king of the land or the issued decree, but were in consecrated and humble respect to the King of Kings. Daniel went home to pray to God - publicly as he had always done.

When the men who petitioned the king to create the

decree witnessed this, they reported it immediately to the king. The king, who loved Daniel, was forced to throw him in the lion's den. In doing so, the king said to Daniel,

"Your God, whom you serve continually, He will deliver you." (15)

The king fasted and suffered through a sleepless night. The king rose early the next day to discover the outcome of Daniel. Miraculously, the lions shut their mouths and did not bother Daniel at all because he believed in God. At the sight of this miracle, the king himself began to worship God and issued a decree that all in his kingdom must honor God as well! He also ordered the men and the families of those who accused Daniel to be thrown into the lion's den. They were immediately torn to pieces by the lions.

We become men and women after God's own heart when we seek and obey him in all situations. When we openly recognize the Lord as the reigning authority in our lives, as our sovereign Savior and ruler over all, he goes out of his way to bring glory to his name, protecting us and shining a light on all that we do in his might. By the power of the Holy Spirit, we embody a 'nevertheless, thy will be done' lifestyle.

Prayer

Most Gracious and Heavenly Father,

Thank you for your unconditional love, mercy, and grace. May the words of our mouths and the meditations of our hearts be pleasing in your sight, Lord, our Rock and our Redeemer. [1] *For all things are permissible but not everything is beneficial. Everything is permissible but not everything is edifying.* [2] *Therefore, seeing we also are surrounded by a great cloud of witnesses, let us lay aside every weight, and the sin which so easily besets us, and let us run with patience the race that is set before us, looking unto Jesus, the author and finisher of our faith, who for the joy that was set before Him endured the cross, despising the shame, and is set down at the right hand of the throne of God.* [3]

You are the living God, and steadfast forever. Your kingdom is the one which shall not be destroyed, and your dominion shall endure to the end. You deliver and rescue, and work signs and wonders in heaven

and on earth. You are he who delivered Daniel from the power of the lions. (16)

In Jesus' Name,

Amen

In the Middle

He stood between the living and the dead, and the plague stopped.

Numbers 16:48

There are times when God will call us to stand in the gap and protect those who do not realize they need to be protected. God does this for us all the time, protecting us from dangers unseen. He is constantly on the throne praying for us. Our God never sleeps.

As we dedicate our lives to doing his will, we become more like him. As ambassadors of Christ, we are called to stand in the middle. Even when God has decided to render a verdict, we can pray for those who hurt us. We can pray for those whose intentions were to destroy us. We are to stand in the gap.

Three Israelite leaders, Korah, Dothan & Abiathar, journeyed with Moses and Aaron from Egypt and settled in the wilderness. As Moses and Aaron received explicit instructions from God, they shared them with the community. But the three men despised their leadership and challenged their ability and authority to lead them. The three of them convinced 250 more of Israel's leaders to echo their voice of opposition.

At the hearing of such accusations, Moses fell into a position of consecrated worship. He then shared with them that their opposition was not to their authority or leadership, but their argument was with God who'd appointed him and

Aaron.

The men did not care. They insisted that not only did Moses and Aaron drag them from a good life, but also promised a good life and had only delivered hardship and toil in the wilderness. They were upset and did not trust the men.

So, Moses told the men to meet them the next day to worship and that all would witness whom God honored as true leadership. All three of the men and the 250 that followed them arrived the next day with their censors filled, ready to worship. The assembly of Israelites watched closely.

Just as God was about to destroy the men, their followers, and the assembly in attendance Moses again fell facedown in consecrated worship and begged God to have mercy on the people. God instructed the people to separate themselves from the three men and 250 leaders that followed them. They did.

Then Moses presented the burden of proof to the people who were unsure of what to believe. He told them that if God truly appointed him and Aaron, then the three leaders would die an unnatural death. Immediately, the three men and their families' homes were swallowed by the earth, then the earth closed completely over them.

Moments later, God consumed the 250 leaders who'd followed them with fire, leaving only the silver vessels used to worship and their charred bodies at the altar.

The following day the people were angry with Moses and Aaron which angered God. God vowed to destroy the people. Immediately, Moses and Aaron fell face down in worship once more. After, Moses instructed Aaron to run and atone for their sins because God had begun to send the plague among them. Aaron went quickly to stand in the middle but not before almost 15,000 were killed.

In the chapter preceding Numbers 16, God had given Moses and Aaron explicit instructions to share with the community about atonement as a community when they sinned unknowingly. Rather than embrace what was being taught, the people rebelled against it and accused the messengers of maleficence.

In teaching the community what to do, God was also preparing Moses and Aaron of their unique responsibility as spiritual leadership. On multiple occasions, they fell in worship to protect those who did not know they needed protection from the wrath of God.

We too are placed in a unique situation in which we are to bless those who do not treat us well, respect us or even honor the God that we serve. We are to pray for them just as God prays for us. We were not always saved and sanctified. We have all lived a season of our lives without God as our head. It was by the mercy, grace and prayers of those who love us that helped us make it to the other side.

We are called to stand in the middle, our prayers can save someone's life and enable them to stand in the middle for others. By the power of the Holy Spirit, we embody a 'nevertheless, thy will be done' lifestyle.

Prayer

Most Gracious and Heavenly Father,

Thank you for your unconditional love, mercy, and grace. May the words of our mouths and the meditations of our hearts be pleasing in your sight, Lord, our Rock and our Redeemer. (1) *For all things are permissible but not everything is beneficial. Everything is permissible but not everything is edifying.* (2) *Therefore, seeing we also are surrounded by a great cloud of witnesses, let us lay aside every weight, and the sin which so easily besets us, and let us run with patience the race that is set before us, looking unto Jesus, the author and finisher of our faith, who for the joy that was set before Him endured the cross, despising the shame, and is set down at the right hand of the throne of God.* (3)

We choose to love our enemies, and do good to those who hate us, bless those who curse us, and pray for those who mistreat us. If someone slaps us on one cheek, we turn to them the other also. If someone takes our coats, we do not withhold our shirts from them. We give to everyone who asks us, and if anyone takes what belongs to us, we do not demand it back. We do to others as we would have them do to us. If we love those who love us, what credit is that to us? Even sinners love those who love them. And if we do good to those who are good to us, what credit is that to us? Even sinners do that. And if we lend to those from whom we expect repayment, what credit is that to us? Even sinners lend to sinners, expecting to be repaid in full. But we love our enemies, do good to them, and lend to them without expecting to get anything back. Then our reward will be great, and we will be children of the Most High, because he is kind to the ungrateful and wicked. We are merciful, just as our Father is merciful. (17)

In Jesus' Name,

Amen

I Decrease as God Increases

Rejoice in the Lord always. I will say it again: Rejoice!
Philippians 4:4

The sincere goal of any person led by Christ is to live a life that is pleasing to God so that his love, wisdom, and purpose may be accomplished through our living. This only occurs when we call on him and listen for his voice. God is faithful. He knows every situation we face, and he understands the complexity and the resulting anxiety that exists and persists in a fight for our attention. Fear is a distraction to keep us from honoring God and doing our best. The enemy will never give up his territory without a fight. Stay in faith.

Paul wrote a letter to the Philippians sharing what he discovered about living a life that honors God first. This life does not place comfort or self-gain at the center. Instead, it proposes the work of God at the center and allows God to guide us.

When we let God guide, we may have to suffer for a season. This is a reality that Paul learned was part of the process. As a Jewish leader, Paul had access to everything his heart desired. He was favored, in power, and could exact punishment on any man with a simple justification of the law.

But when Paul met Jesus, his life changed dramatically. As a Christian leader, he understood those he once persecuted. Paul availed himself to become a willing vessel of Christ because he experienced the supernatural revelation of

Christ.

As followers of Christ, this is something we each uniquely understand. Christ reveals his true nature to us, in a way that opens our understanding. While we had ears and could hear what members of the church would say to us, we did not understand. While we witnessed the activities of the members of the church, we could not understand its true purpose. Our lens of understanding was warped by selfish ambition and material wealth, status, and power. While these are not evil attributes or altogether bad in nature, it is the relentless pursuit of such that will make good people compromise their morals and convictions for gain. When we each experience our personal road to Damascus (when Paul's eyes were opened) we can see ourselves and our past activities more clearly.

Paul's imprisonment served the purpose in helping us all to understand what could be gained at our personal cost of suffering. He learned that unity, confidence in God, learning through Godly example, and rejoicing when God uses us for his glory are a benefit to the kingdom.

We are on earth preparing to live an eternal life with God in heaven. The temptations and desires that exist before us today may exponentially increase in the hereafter. Therefore, we must stand on a solid foundation of trusting, believing and honoring the will of God before all else, as the issues of all life flow from God.

By the power of the Holy Spirit, we embody a 'nevertheless, thy will be done' lifestyle.

Prayer

Most Gracious and Heavenly Father,

Thank you for your unconditional love, mercy, and grace. May the words of our mouths and the meditations of our hearts be pleasing in your sight, Lord, our Rock and our Redeemer. (1) For all things are permissible but not everything is beneficial. Everything is permissible but not everything is edifying. (2) Therefore, seeing we also are surrounded by a great cloud of witnesses, let us lay aside every weight, and the sin which so easily besets us, and let us run with patience the race that is set before us, looking unto Jesus, the author and finisher of our faith, who for the joy that was set before Him endured the cross, despising the shame, and is set down at the right hand of the throne of God. (3)

And this is our prayer: that our love may abound more and more in knowledge and depth of insight, so that we may be able to discern what is best and may be pure and blameless for the day of Christ, filled with the fruit of righteousness that comes through Jesus Christ—to the glory and praise of God. (18)

In Jesus' Name,

Amen

Stand

Now Stephen, a man full of God's grace and power, performed great wonders and signs among the people. Opposition arose, however, from members of the Synagogue of the Freedmen (as it was called)—Jews of Cyrene and Alexandria as well as the provinces of Cilicia and Asia—who began to argue with Stephen. But they could not stand up against the wisdom the Spirit gave him as he spoke. Then they secretly persuaded some men to say, "We have heard Stephen speak blasphemous words against Moses and against God."

Acts 6:8-11

Sin bears no owner, it simply exists. It is the dark matter, the black hole, it seeks to consume, to destroy, to rid the atmosphere of everything creative, wonderful and good. Sin can be found in the best of people, even those who are commissioned to do a great work for God.

When the innocent find themselves in the crosshairs of darkness, it can be difficult to find our way out... no matter how hard we try, or how concise our argument may be. This is when we are called to simply, stand.

Stephen was a man of God doing the work of God to the best of his ability. His co-workers became jealous and devised a way to diminish his character. They solicited false witnesses to testify against him and make untrue accusations.

Stephen was placed on trial and forced to testify of his actions. His eloquent testimony detailed the intimate relationship between God and man, including the pinnacle of his great love for us through the revelation and untimely death of Jesus Christ. He shared the beautiful power of love available to all through the power of the Holy Spirit. And finalized his speech with a poignant plea to God to forgive those who would persecute him.

Stephen prayed for his enemies and was stoned to death. But one of the men who approved of his stoning death saw it as a beacon and open door to persecute all of the followers of Jesus. His name was Saul, a devout Jew, and he went home to home to find Christians and persecute them. But Stephen's prayer for God to forgive his enemies was his last miracle. Because one day, Jesus Christ revealed himself to Saul, the persecutor of the Christians, and converted him to become an ambassador of Christ, first to the Gentiles and eventually the Jews.

Stephen's living was not in vain. His death served a greater purpose. When it was time to face his accusers, he stood in faith, with conviction and grit. He faced his accusers with truth in his mouth, love in his heart, and trust in God to deliver him to his next destination. As he was stoned, Stephen saw God and Jesus in heaven, and he went to sleep.

Like Stephen, we all face unfair and unjust situations. Rather than be angry, we must be willing to forgive and trust God for our next destination. Our living has not been in vain.

By the power of the Holy Spirit, we embody a 'nevertheless, thy will be done' lifestyle.

Prayer

Most Gracious and Heavenly Father,

Thank you for your unconditional love, mercy, and grace. May the words of our mouths and the meditations of our hearts be pleasing in your sight, Lord, our Rock and our Redeemer. (1) For all things are permissible but not everything is beneficial. Everything is permissible but not everything is edifying. (2) Therefore, seeing we also are surrounded by a great cloud of witnesses, let us lay aside every weight, and the sin which so easily besets us, and let us run with patience the race that is set before us, looking unto Jesus, the author and finisher of our faith, who for the joy that was set before Him endured the cross, despising the shame, and is set down at the right hand of the throne of God. (3)

Finally, we are strong in the Lord and in his mighty power. We put on the full armor of God, so that we can take our stand against the devil's schemes. For our struggle is not against flesh and blood, but against the rulers, against the authorities, against the powers of this dark world and against the spiritual forces of evil in the heavenly realms. Therefore we put on the full armor of God, so that when the day of evil comes, we may be able to stand our ground, and after we have done everything, to stand. We stand firm then, with the belt of truth buckled around our waist, with the breastplate of righteousness in place, and with our feet fitted with the readiness that comes from the gospel of peace. In addition to all this, we take up the shield of faith, with which we can extinguish all the flaming arrows of the evil one. We take the helmet of salvation and the sword of the Spirit, which is the word of God. And we pray in the Spirit on all occasions with all kinds of prayers and requests. With this in mind, we are alert and always keep on praying for all the Lord's people. We pray also for those who preach and teach the gospel, that whenever they speak, words may be given to them so that they will fearlessly make known the mystery of the gospel, for which we are each ambassadors. We pray that we all may declare it fearlessly, as we should. (19)

In Jesus' Name,

Amen

Recognizing the Spirit of the Lord

The two angels arrived at Sodom in the evening, and Lot was sitting in the gateway of the city. When he saw them, he got up to meet them and bowed down with his face to the ground. "My lords," he said, "please turn aside to your servant's house. You can wash your feet and spend the night and then go on your way early in the morning."

Genesis 19:1-2

God responds to the cries of his people. He is thorough in his investigation and God is no respecter of persons. He is going to not only inspect those who are accused of wrongdoing but he is also going to inspect those who cried out and those who are witnesses.

When the angels of the Lord arrived to inspect the evil going on in Sodom and Gomorrah, they stopped at Abraham and Sarah's house prior to destroying it.

From the moment Abraham saw them, he was very hospitable. He bowed down to them in respect, as he recognized they were angels. He offered to wash their feet, feed them, and asked them to stay and rest awhile.

They did exactly as he asked. After they had eaten and rested, Abraham walked with them. Then they decided amongst themselves that they wanted to reveal to Abraham what they were about to do in destroying the neighboring city.

Abraham immediately pleaded for the lives of the innocent, as he knew his nephew Lot was there and believed that he would be found to be a good man if measured.

The angels agreed that if they found at least ten righteous people in the land of Sodom and Gomorrah they would not destroy it. Abraham then left them to do their will.

Upon entering Sodom, Abraham's nephew Lot was sitting at the gate, ready and waiting to welcome them. When they entered, he immediately bowed with his face to the ground, welcomed them, offered to wash their feet, and give them a place to rest. But the angels responded they would rather spend the night in the square of town. But Lot knew that evil was waiting for them and he persisted in his insistence that they reside with him for the evening. The angels agreed and before they could get into Lot's home and secure it, the men of the city were at the door beckoning the visitors to be released.

Lot knew evil was in their hearts and earnestly pleaded with the men. He even offered his two virgin daughters to them. The angels struck the men with blindness and told Lot to gather his family and prepare to leave the town; they were going to destroy it.

God is a witness to everything that happens. He never sleeps nor slumbers. He hears our every cry and recognizes our situation. He will send relief to those in need.

Because Abraham and Lot recognized the angels of God, Lot's life and the lives of his family members were saved. They not only recognized the Spirit of God, but they gave him honor and respect. We never know when we are entertaining angels, unaware. Fortunately, God has given each of us wisdom and discernment and we have the ability to try the spirit by the spirit. This means a good person will have good fruit, a way that their goodness can be revealed through the work of their hands and the measure of their heart (in how they treat others). Along the same lines, we must do our best to treat every person with honor, respect, and dignity.

By the power of the Holy Spirit, we embody a

'nevertheless, thy will be done' lifestyle.

Prayer

Most Gracious and Heavenly Father,

Thank you for your unconditional love, mercy, and grace. May the words of our mouths and the meditations of our hearts be pleasing in your sight, Lord, our Rock and our Redeemer. (1) For all things are permissible but not everything is beneficial. Everything is permissible but not everything is edifying. (2) Therefore, seeing we also are surrounded by a great cloud of witnesses, let us lay aside every weight, and the sin which so easily besets us, and let us run with patience the race that is set before us, looking unto Jesus, the author and finisher of our faith, who for the joy that was set before Him endured the cross, despising the shame, and is set down at the right hand of the throne of God. (3)

The Lord is good to all; he has compassion on all he has made. All your works praise you, Lord; your faithful people extol you. They tell of the glory of your kingdom and speak of your might, so that all people may know of your mighty acts and the glorious splendor of your kingdom. Your kingdom is an everlasting kingdom, and your dominion endures through all generations. The Lord is trustworthy in all he promises and faithful in all he does. The Lord upholds all who fall and lifts up all who are bowed down. The eyes of all look to you, and you give them their food at the proper time. You open your hand and satisfy the desires of every living thing. The Lord is righteous in all his ways and faithful in all he does. The Lord is near to all who call on him, to all who call on him in truth. He fulfills the desires of those who fear him; he hears their cry and saves them. The Lord watches over all who love him, but all the wicked he will destroy. Our mouths will speak in praise of the Lord. Let every creature praise his holy name for ever and ever. (20)

In Jesus' Name,

Amen

At the Command of God

Then Jesus said to the centurion, "Go! Let it be done just as you believed it would." And his servant was healed at that moment.

Matthew 8:13

Everything that we say, think, and believe matters. We were born to create. God is the creator of all things and in his likeness, we have been gifted with imagination, will, and the ability to pursue with tenacity, fortitude, perseverance and strength. What we believe either negates, stagnates or generates action. Out of the abundance of our hearts, we speak.

For several years, I worked for a car reservation agency. During this experience, phone representatives received what were called, QA calls or quality assurance calls. Over a short amount of time, one could always recognize a QA call from the moment the call began. The most glaring way to recognize that a call was simply a test of quality assurance was that the tone and substance of authenticity was absent. Friendly gestures were either non-existent or were glaringly overt and uncomfortable. Every jot and tittle of responsible communication was met as though someone were checking off boxes as they spoke. Genuine pleas for help, assistance, and need for your services were replaced with general platitudes and polite gratitude. One could easily recognize a QA call from all other calls because they were strikingly different than the abundance of calls you received day in and day out. Real customers need help. Therefore, people in need speak with sincerity and without alternative objectives. They are not trying to measure an emoticon of different responses to different scenarios. In real conversations, trust can be developed in a short amount of time to ensure everyone involved is able to get what is needed quickly and efficiently. A real customer is also sincerely grateful for the service you provide.

Matthew chapter 8 allows us to see a day in the life of Jesus as a healer and commander of blessings. From a man with leprosy that simply asked if Jesus was willing to heal him, to a commander filled with faith whose servant was sick far away, to a woman too bowed down with fever to ask for her healing, to his disciples filled with fear during a ferocious storm, to violent and demon-possessed men terrorizing a territory - at the command of Jesus all of them were healed.

Here in lies the difference, those who truly need help are genuine in their communications and their words flow from the heart. They sincerely need help and will call out to God in spirit and truth, seeking him to protect, guide and heal them. God who is faithful and sees the heart clearly, responds by speaking a word of deliverance to help in a time of need.

We must have enough faith to call on God, to believe that God is willing to heal us, and trust that at the command of his word, his will shall be done.

By the power of the Holy Spirit, we embody a 'nevertheless, thy will be done' lifestyle.

Prayer

Most Gracious and Heavenly Father,

Thank you for your unconditional love, mercy, and grace. May the words of our mouths and the meditations of our hearts be pleasing in your sight, Lord, our Rock and our Redeemer. (1) For all things are permissible but not everything is beneficial. Everything is permissible but not everything is edifying. (2) Therefore, seeing we also are surrounded by a great cloud of witnesses, let us lay aside every weight, and the sin which so easily besets us, and let us run with patience the race that is set before us, looking unto Jesus, the author and finisher of our faith, who for the joy that was set before Him endured the cross, despising the shame, and is set down at the right hand of the throne of God. (3)

Therefore, since we are surrounded by such a great cloud of witnesses, let us throw off everything that hinders and the sin that so easily entangles. And let us run with perseverance the race marked out for us, fixing our eyes on Jesus, the pioneer and perfecter of faith. For the joy set before him he endured the cross, scorning its shame, and sat down at the right hand of the throne of God. We consider him who endured such opposition from sinners, so that we will not grow weary and lose heart. (21)

In Jesus' Name,

Amen

Real Love

And being found in appearance as a man, he humbled himself by becoming obedient to death—even death on a cross!

Philippians 2:8

I would do just about anything for my children. When I say no, and from time to time I do; it is painful. I want to give my children everything their heart desires, but I know they are not prepared for everything they want or that I may want to give them. It pains me to hear the disappointment (or other range of emotions expressed) in their voice when they accept that I cannot be of assistance. But my kids know, mama is here and will always be here as God allows. Real love is a two-way street. It gives and it takes; it begs mercy and gives mercy… but it never ever goes away. Real love is forever.

Jesus gave generously of himself to all who walk the earth. From the creation of the earth and all that lived within it, to the limited-scope destruction of life on the earth and we the descendants of those who survived it. Jesus has and will consistently serve as the author and finisher of our faith.

Jesus also has a heart of gold. He loves us more than words can express and seeks to bless us with his spirit, companionship, protection, provision, love, and wisdom. Jesus seeks to have a relationship with each of us. He never gives up on us. He stands at the doors of our hearts, knocking, knocking, and knocking, hoping we will open the door.

Jesus left heaven to ensure we have a clear path to get there because he desires that we experience abundant lives.

There is an enemy that hopes he can convince us that heaven isn't beautiful and that God isn't wonderful. His goal is to kill, steal and destroy.

Jesus has allowed humanity to drink from his well of wisdom, pull from his power to be healed, tap into his abundant resources to be blessed, and watched them walk away as he was accused, beaten and ultimately murdered. Jesus gave us his all. So much so, that even at this very moment, he prays for us without ceasing. He governs over our lives with justice, mercy, and grace.

As a parent, we try to give our children space to learn their way. Sometimes, they have to feel around in the dark to appreciate the light. They have to lean back on what they learned by observance, experience, and education to make wise decisions. They will grow up and become, just as we have grown to become. We have the opportunity and responsibility to watch, assist, and glow over every achievement, every fall, and every moment of uncertainty. Our love for our children is authentic and filled with hope for a beautiful future.

In the same way, Jesus has kept an eye on us, the chastisement of our peace is upon him, yet he has never complained. He has never pointed a finger at us and proclaimed, "You did this to me." He doesn't require that we atone for our sins day in and day out. No, he defeated sin and death in one fell swoop when he sacrificed his life for ours.

Therefore, let us, as ambassadors of Christ, reflect his humility and grace with excellence. Let us serve others as Christ has served each of us to help others see the love of Christ through our consistent ability to respond to offense with love, mercy, and grace as Christ so loved us.

We must suture our lips, be still and quiet, that we may hear God's heart on the matter prior to responding from a place of offense, anger, or pain. We must love others the way Christ has loved us and let us do so cheerfully, knowing we are good stewards of the time, knowledge, wisdom, and faith God has so freely given us.

Mary J. Blige sings a song called, "Real Love." The lyrics sing of someone searching for authentic love and how it is mandatory she finds it. In the same way, there are people walking this earth searching for an authentic relationship that leads to real love. This is a space that only God can occupy. Others may get close, but no other love can reach the depths that God can. For some, the only way they may experience Christ's love is through our consistency of action despite how we are treated.

When we show up and smile through the pain, they are able to witness the humility of Christ through us. When we give and give and give of ourselves without grumbling or complaining, we are extending the generosity of God. When we forgive, forgive, and forgive, again and again, we are creating a space for conversation, revelation, and restoration through the example of grace empowered by the Holy Spirit. It is not a weakness to give in this way, it is strength personified with a specific goal in mind, to reflect the 'real love' we have so freely been given.

By the power of the Holy Spirit, we embody a 'nevertheless, thy will be done' lifestyle.

Prayer

Most Gracious and Heavenly Father,

Thank you for your unconditional love, mercy, and grace. May the words of our mouths and the meditations of our hearts be pleasing in your sight, Lord, our Rock and our Redeemer. (1) For all things are permissible but not everything is beneficial. Everything is permissible but not everything is edifying. (2) Therefore, seeing we also are surrounded by a great cloud of witnesses, let us lay aside every weight, and the sin which so easily besets us, and let us run with patience the race that is set before us, looking unto Jesus, the author and finisher of our faith, who for the joy that was set before Him endured the cross, despising the shame, and is set down at the right hand of the throne of God. (3)

Therefore if we have any encouragement from being united with Christ, if any comfort from his love, if any common sharing in the Spirit, if any tenderness and compassion, then let us make our joy complete by being like-minded, having the same love, being one in spirit and of one mind. We deny selfish ambition and vain conceit. Rather, in humility, we value others above ourselves, not looking to your own interests but each of us to the interests of the others. In our relationships with one another, we are committed to have the same mindset as Christ Jesus. (22)

In Jesus' Name,

Amen

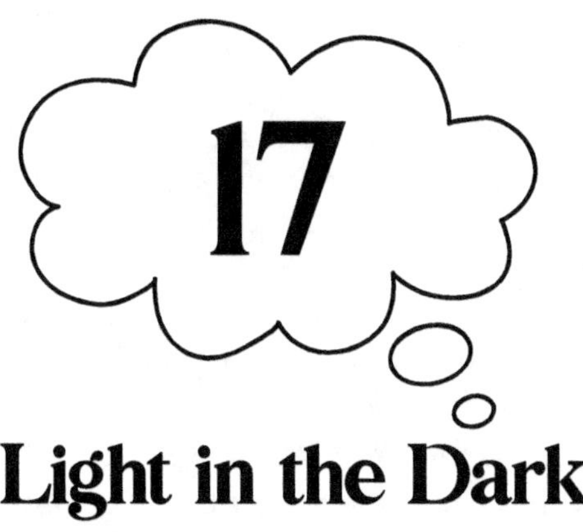

Light in the Dark

Nabal answered David's servants, "Who is this David? Who is this son of Jesse? Many servants are breaking away from their masters these days. Why should I take my bread and water, and the meat I have slaughtered for my shearers, and give it to men coming from who knows where?"

I Samuel 25:10-11

We may do what is right, when it is right, for those who are not right. When our goodwill is met with opposition, disrespect, and total disregard instead of appreciation and reciprocity; retribution and revenge may seem reasonable and due.

David was a man of war, yet obedient and respectful to God. He was generous and wise, discerning, and intentional. After the death of Samuel, a man who anointed David to be king, and after he'd escaped the many attempts by King Saul to kill him, David and six hundred of his men camped in the Desert of Paran.

In the desert, the shepherds of a man named Nabal, were tending their flocks for a season. David, being a shepherd and fully understanding the value of protecting the sheep, used his servants to form a circle of protection around the men, preventing any loss.

At the end of the season, when it was time to celebrate, David sent several of his men to request a gift of gratitude, whatever Nabal (a man of great increase) could spare, for he and his men.

Instead, Nabal insulted the men and sent them away with nothing. He also made disrespectful comments about David, insinuating that he was a disobedient servant to his master (meaning Saul, the king determined to kill David). This response sent David into a rage. He was ready to kill Nabal. Nabal did not only appreciate David's gift of protection, but he also added insult to injury by insinuating that David was not even deserving of his respect.

One of Nabal's shepherds went to Abigail, Nabal's wife, and explained the matter. He shared that they were only protected because of David and his circle of men, who were there day in and day out to keep them safe. Abigail also knew who David was and she immediately went into action. She gathered a great meal for him and his men and sent it ahead of her with her servants. Then she arrived and met David, face-to-face. Abigail apologized to David, pronounced a blessing of protection, cursed his enemies, and prophesied he would soon become king. Finally, Abigail asked him to remember her.

When Abigail returned home, her husband was partying - drunk and living it up as though he had nothing to lose. The next morning, Abigail told her husband what she'd done. He immediately suffered a heart attack and eventually succumbed to his injury. David heard about his fate, thanked God for enacting vengeance, and sent for Abigail to become his wife. She gratefully and gracefully submitted to his request.

Our anger for those who make a mockery of the good we perform for their benefit may be justified and warranted, but we will not have to take revenge or avenge ourselves. Vengeance belongs to God, and he is faithful to repay. Not only will he repay it, but he will allow us to bear witness to their destruction. Likewise, when we have given our all despite our need and those we serve refuse to acknowledge it, God will send our blessings through other avenues. Just as David did not take revenge on his enemies (Saul or Nabal), we too are to stay in faith, believing that God is aware, God will avenge, and God will provide.

By the power of the Holy Spirit, we embody a 'nevertheless, thy will be done' lifestyle.

Prayer

Most Gracious and Heavenly Father,

Thank you for your unconditional love, mercy, and grace. May the words of our mouths and the meditations of our hearts be pleasing in your sight, Lord, our Rock and our Redeemer. (1) For all things are permissible but not everything is beneficial. Everything is permissible but not everything is edifying. (2) Therefore, seeing we also are surrounded by a great cloud of witnesses, let us lay aside every weight, and the sin which so easily besets us, and let us run with patience the race that is set before us, looking unto Jesus, the author and finisher of our faith, who for the joy that was set before Him endured the cross, despising the shame, and is set down at the right hand of the throne of God. (3)

The Lord is our shepherd, we do not want. He makes us lie down in green pastures, he leads us beside quiet waters, he refreshes our souls. He guides us along the right paths for his name's sake. Even though we walk through the darkest valley, we will fear no evil, for your are with us; your rod and your staff, they comfort us. You prepare a table before us in the presence of our enemies. You anoint our head with oil; our cup overflows. Surely your goodness and love will follow us all the days of our lives, and we will dwell in the house of the Lord forever. (23) Therefore, let our light so shine before men that they see our good works, and glorify our Father in heaven. (24)

In Jesus' Name,

Amen

Do Everything Well

People were overwhelmed with amazement. "He has done everything well," they said. "He even makes the deaf hear and the mute speak."

Mark 7:36

This life can often feel like a survival of the fittest, and quite honestly, it is. Our lives are often measured by the thoughts we share, words we speak, and actions we take. If those three areas of our lives are centered around Godly love: compassion, kindness, humility, honesty, service, and connection, we can usually survive the strongest of storms. But it is only when we are personally committed and accountable to God through faith, connection, honor and service that we can be viewed as one who does everything well.

And they exceeded our expectations: They gave themselves first of all to the Lord, and then by the will of God also to us. (25)

When Jesus fed the four thousand, there was a large crowd that listened to him speak for more than three days without a meal. That is amazing. I don't think there is anyone walking this earth, at this time, that I would be willing to sit and listen to for more than three days without a lunch break or a meal.

When I read the snippets of conversations Jesus had with the large groups that he and his disciples traveled to visit, I am empowered and encouraged to apply the wisdom he shared with them to my life and to the lives of those God has allowed me to influence. As John says in chapter 21, it is simply impossible to capture all what Jesus shared or the miracles he performed.

So when I stop to process and realize that a crowd, more poignantly a large crowd of four thousand people, sat listening to Jesus for three days without a meal… I know Jesus was filling them with an abundance of knowledge that hit them in their hearts, simply because he knows us.

After which, Jesus miraculously takes what he is given, seven loaves of bread and a few fish, to feed them before sending the large crowd home because he did not want them to become ill on their way due to a lack of sustenance.

Our faith in God is what fuels our desire and ability to serve God and be accountable to him. During this season of Jesus' life, he was not only sharing the gospel, but he was preparing his disciples to continue the work after he transcended. The disciples needed to believe, have faith, and trust God just as much as any other believer in order to do the work God has prepared them to do. Otherwise, they were simply fans of Jesus and not his disciples.

After they fed the four thousand and began to travel, the disciples realized they were about to embark on a long journey across the sea and they did not bring anything with them except one loaf of bread. Their bewilderment irritated Jesus. Jesus warned them not to be like the Pharisees, who after witnessing a miracle asked for one. Instead, they were to believe and know that God will always make a way. Jesus asked them how many baskets of bread were left over after they fed the crowd. He wanted them to consider that what they were left with is what they began with, nothing missing - all that was needed God supplied.

Another note to consider is that while all the bread supplied was returned, it was returned broken and fragmented. When God is preparing us to be a gift, he will first break us and then put us back together. That is to say that until we experience a level of brokenness that cannot be described and it is subsequently healed by God, we do not fully learn to trust God with our most vulnerable situations, and therefore cannot teach others that they too can trust him when they are most vulnerable. It is when a father brings their child to be healed, or a woman who is about to eat her last meal and die, or a friend that only wishes for his friend to walk, hear or be healed that in a desperate plea and seed of faith, turn to Jesus and beg for help, a believer is made.

After Jesus was baptized, he was sent into the wilderness for forty days and nights without food or water, and tempted by Satan on multiple occasions. Afterwards, he was able to preach the gospel to many. Jesus said it best when he shared,

"Whoever wants to be my disciple must deny themselves and take up their cross and follow me. For whoever wants to save their life will lose it, but whoever loses their life for me and for the gospel will save it. What good is it for someone to gain the whole world, yet forfeit their soul? Or what can anyone give in exchange for their soul? If anyone is ashamed of me and my words in this adulterous and sinful generation, the Son of Man will be ashamed of them when he comes in his Father's glory with the holy angels." (26)

The process is just as important as the results. If we do not adhere to God's formula, we can do something good without accomplishing his will or his purpose, therefore missing the opportunity to do everything well.

By the power of the Holy Spirit, we embody a 'nevertheless, thy will be done' lifestyle.

Prayer

Most Gracious and Heavenly Father,

Thank you for your unconditional love, mercy, and grace. May the words of our mouths and the meditations of our hearts be pleasing in your sight, Lord, our Rock and our Redeemer. (1) For all things are permissible but not everything is beneficial. Everything is permissible but not everything is edifying. (2) Therefore, seeing we also are surrounded by a great cloud of witnesses, let us lay aside every weight, and the sin which so easily besets us, and let us run with patience the race that is set before us, looking unto Jesus, the author and finisher of our faith, who for the joy that was set before Him endured the cross, despising the shame, and is set down at the right hand of the throne of God. (3)

Create in us a pure heart, O God, and renew a steadfast spirit within us. Do not cast us from your presence or take your Holy Spirit from us. Restore to us the joy of your salvation and grant us a willing spirit, to sustain us. Then we will teach transgressors your ways, so that sinners will turn back to you. Deliver us from the guilt of bloodshed, O God, you who are God our Savior, and our tongue will sing of your righteousness. Open our lips, Lord, and our mouths will declare your praise. You do not delight in sacrifice, or we would bring it; you do not take pleasure in burnt offerings. Our sacrifice, O God, are broken spirits; broken and contrite hearts you, God, will not despise. May it please you to prosper Zion, to build up the walls of Jerusalem. Then you will delight in the sacrifices of the righteous, in burnt offerings offered whole; then bulls will be offered on your altar. (27)

In Jesus' Name,

Amen

Forgive & Let God Repay

Anyone who does wrong will be repaid for their wrongs, and there is no favoritism.

Colossians 3:25

Our lives can be littered with people who mistreat us and walk with the intention of harming us. If we are not careful, some of the worst situations we've experienced will echo over time. Anything that echoes amplifies and eventually causes a root of bitterness in our hearts. But Jesus died so that we could enjoy life.

Jesus teaches us to live intentionally, placing God first and love at the center of all we do. We are to place God's will above our own and live like it is heaven on earth. When we live a life that truly honors God, we begin to enjoy life. A life filled with caring for others, being generous, and allowing the purpose of our work to become our greatest desire (rather than the tangible rewards or acknowledgement from those who assigned it), which will certainly lead to a more fulfilling life.

Likewise, we must be willing to leave behind anything else that may keep us from living our best life, such as a pursuit of specific desires (sex, money, power, fame, addictions, etc.) and turning away from offense (anger, rage, ill will, etc.) can help us to focus more on the adventures obedience to God affords us. When God can trust us, he will send us to new places, expand our territory, and introduce us in spaces we never thought we would be in.

Finally, we must learn to forgive others. We have all experienced forgiveness and mercy from God for our sins, and God is faithful to forgive. Therefore, as ambassadors of Christ, and recipients of his mercy, we must also acknowledge that it is also our responsibility to forgive. I know how painful and difficult it can be to forgive someone who intentionally hurt you and learn to trust them again. But rather than trust them, trust God who sees your efforts and rewards those who attempt to live a life that pleases him. While the person may or may not change, the goal is for us to change how we process, respond to, and hold on to offenses. God is sovereign, there is nothing anyone can do that he will not take care of. Vengeance belongs to him.

By the power of the Holy Spirit, we embody a 'nevertheless, thy will be done' lifestyle.

Prayer

Most Gracious and Heavenly Father,

Thank you for your unconditional love, mercy, and grace. May the words of our mouths and the meditations of our hearts be pleasing in your sight, Lord, our Rock and our Redeemer. (1) For all things are permissible but not everything is beneficial. Everything is permissible but not everything is edifying. (2) Therefore, seeing we also are surrounded by a great cloud of witnesses, let us lay aside every weight, and the sin which so easily besets us, and let us run with patience the race that is set before us, looking unto Jesus, the author and finisher of our faith, who for the joy that was set before Him endured the cross, despising the shame, and is set down at the right hand of the throne of God. (3)

Therefore it is an honor to live a life worthy of the calling we have received. We will do our best to always be completely humble and gentle; patient, bearing with one another in love. We make every effort to keep the unity of the Spirit through the bond of peace. There is o ne body and one Spirit, just as we were called to one hope when we were called; one Lord, one faith, one baptism; one God and Father of all, who is over all and through all and in all. But to each one of us grace has been given as Christ apportioned it. (28)

In Jesus' Name,
Amen

Intentionality

No one can serve two masters. Either you will hate the one and love the other, or you will be devoted to the one and despise the other. You cannot serve both God and money.

Matthew 6:24

We are filled with desires, hopes, and dreams. There is no doubt that when we wake up every morning, we are geared to perform as heat-seeking missiles, determined to reach our personal goals for the day. Our drive is often fueled by desire or demand.

We each have responsibilities that must be met in order to obtain our goals. Sometimes those responsibilities can feel burdensome or unnecessary, but it is the discipline of showing up, performing, and doing so with consistency that renders the results we desire. Unconsciously, we become what we hope to be.

Honoring God with our lives requires intentionality. It is not happenstance. If we walk around drinking, having sex and cursing; treating others with disrespect and gossiping; doing evil to others or placing selfish desires over God's desires, we cannot honor God. We must also be certain to give in private, and to practice humility concerning our relationship with God. It is to be private, respected and treated as personally important to us.

Therefore, just as we do with any other goal we hope to achieve, we must practice honoring God daily. This is only achieved by placing him first in our lives, tithing when we earn, fasting and praying, and giving to others. Most importantly, we must learn to forgive in order to be forgiven. We all make mistakes and require the grace of God in order to become what he has designed us to be. In letting go of what we want, and embracing what God desires for us, God has a way of exceeding our greatest expectations.

We must learn to let go of our control and let God take the lead. God is faithful and intentional. By the power of the Holy Spirit, we embody a 'nevertheless, thy will be done' lifestyle.

Prayer

Most Gracious and Heavenly Father,

Thank you for your unconditional love, mercy, and grace. May the words of our mouths and the meditations of our hearts be pleasing in your sight, Lord, our Rock and our Redeemer. (1) For all things are permissible but not everything is beneficial. Everything is permissible but not everything is edifying. (2) Therefore, seeing we also are surrounded by a great cloud of witnesses, let us lay aside every weight, and the sin which so easily besets us, and let us run with patience the race that is set before us, looking unto Jesus, the author and finisher of our faith, who for the joy that was set before Him endured the cross, despising the shame, and is set down at the right hand of the throne of God. (3)

Our Father in heaven, hallowed be your name, your kingdom come, your will be done, on earth as it is in heaven. Give us today our daily bread. And forgive us our debts, as we also have forgiven our debtors. And lead us not into temptation, but deliver us from the evil one. (29)

In Jesus' Name,

Amen

God is Our Mediator

Moses answered him, "Because the people come to me to seek God's will. Whenever they have a dispute, it is brought to me, and I decide between the parties and inform them of God's decrees and instructions."

Exodus 18:15-16

It is good for us to seek God at all times, but it is wonderful when God sends for those who will help share in our burdens. Those who assist us help us to serve with greater efficiency, productivity, and help to create systems that streamline resources, communication, and workflow.

When we keep God first every morning and choose to align our will with his will, God will assist us in focusing on what is most important. His will is for the betterment of all. It helps us to look outside of ourselves and find ways to serve larger audiences with greater efficiency. When we stop making it about us, we can serve others with excellence.

Moses served God with a humble heart keeping God's will first. The people recognized this trait and would bring their grievances to him to help adjudicate justice according to the will of God. But the need exceeded his bandwidth and capacity to serve. His father-in-law witnessed the burden it was placing on him and suggested a system that would allow Moses to exponentially increase the will of God to others in a great way.

Jethro taught Moses to select staff that were God-fearing, moral and could make sound judgments. He shared that Moses should teach them how he preferred for court to be held and gave them the freedom to make those decisions. Moses would only see cases that were too complex or difficult to judge so that God's ultimate will could be delivered in all cases.

God is our mediator. It is not about us, our authority, ability, or admiration - it is about God and the love he wishes to share with all. By the power of the Holy Spirit, we embody a 'nevertheless, thy will be done' lifestyle.

Prayer

Most Gracious and Heavenly Father,

Thank you for your unconditional love, mercy, and grace. May the words of our mouths and the meditations of our hearts be pleasing in your sight, Lord, our Rock and our Redeemer. (1) For all things are permissible but not everything is beneficial. Everything is permissible but not everything is edifying. (2) Therefore, seeing we also are surrounded by a great cloud of witnesses, let us lay aside every weight, and the sin which so easily besets us, and let us run with patience the race that is set before us, looking unto Jesus, the author and finisher of our faith, who for the joy that was set before Him endured the cross, despising the shame, and is set down at the right hand of the throne of God. (3)

Teach us your way, Lord; lead us in a straight path because of our oppressors. Do not turn us over to the desire of our foes, for false witnesses rise up against us, spouting malicious accusations. We remain confident of this: we will see the goodness of the Lord in the land of the living. We wait for the Lord; are strong and take heart and wait for the Lord. (29)

In Jesus' Name,

Amen

The Last Days

Above all, you must understand that in the last days scoffers will come, scoffing and following their own evil desires.

2 Peter 3:3

Nothing lasts forever. Relationships end; memories have been made and all involved move on. When we look back on history, the characters, and people we have come to admire are no longer here. They have gone on and their most notable moments have been etched in time. We too will one day leave this earth. The story people tell of us depends solely on the choices we make today. More importantly, how we spend eternity depends on what we believe.

"God is not human, that he should lie, not a human being, that he should change his mind. Does he speak and then not act? Does he promise and not fulfill?" (31)

So, the question becomes, 'Do we believe God?' If we believe God, we know that the destruction of our earth will come like a thief in the night, a meteor that no one is able to detect, causing the earth to catch fire and be destroyed. Will we be like the young ladies that did not have oil in their lamps because they assumed they had time?

God is calling us to wake up every day with his will and his purpose in mind. He is calling us to become everything that he created us to be that we may help others to experience his love and unending mercy and grace.

Our lives on this earth are not about leaving a legacy

that is honored and esteemed, or even an inheritance for our children, it is about ensuring that we have lived our best lives with God that we may live an eternal life of peace in heaven.

Consider this, we pay a tithe of ten percent to God for everything he has given us. If we also are to give a tithe of our time, which equates to the first part of our day, wouldn't a tithe on eternal life be the life we live on earth? That is to imagine that eternal life could be measured… When we look at the galaxy and the stars, at life that is generated around us (trees, oceans, mountains, and more) that is beyond our control, isn't it wise for us to worship the God who created this beautiful world for us to live in? Isn't wise to believe that just as he created it, he could also destroy it?

We are a beautiful workmanship of God, his being, he chose to live and fulfill his will on the earth. It is not just a responsibility to do so, it is an honor! By the power of the Holy Spirit, we embody a 'nevertheless, thy will be done' lifestyle.

Prayer

Most Gracious and Heavenly Father,

Thank you for your unconditional love, mercy, and grace. May the words of our mouths and the meditations of our hearts be pleasing in your sight, Lord, our Rock and our Redeemer. (1) For all things are permissible but not everything is beneficial. Everything is permissible but not everything is edifying. (2) Therefore, seeing we also are surrounded by a great cloud of witnesses, let us lay aside every weight, and the sin which so easily besets us, and let us run with patience the race that is set before us, looking unto Jesus, the author and finisher of our faith, who for the joy that was set before Him endured the cross, despising the shame, and is set down at the right hand of the throne of God. (3)

We praise you because we are fearfully and wonderfully made; your works are wonderful, we know that full well. Our frame was not hidden from you when we were made in the secret place, when we were woven together in the depths of the earth. Your eyes saw our unformed bodies; all the days ordained for us were written in your book before one of them came to be. How precious to us are your thoughts, God! How vast is the sum of them! Were we to count them, they would outnumber the grains of sand—when we awake, we are still with you. (32)

In Jesus' Name,

Amen

Sent

Again Jesus said, "Peace be with you! As the Father has sent me, I am sending you."

John 20:21

Each of our lives is filled with ups and downs, seasons of adventure that none of us could have imagined. We never knew we would grow up and become who we are today. But our journeys are no surprise to God. Our paths were ordained and orchestrated that we may become all that God has called us to be. While many of us are called, a few of us are chosen.

Jesus was ordained to become the Savior of the world. Despite the revelation of this future being revealed in scripture, his disciples who walked with him and learned from him, were still not fully aware of his destiny. Like the disciples, we never know why God is taking us a specific way in life, but our job is to trust him.

When Jesus was crucified, buried and rose from the grave, Mary, one of his devout followers was devastated to find his grave empty. Jesus came to her and showed her that he was still alive, just in a different way. He told her to tell the disciples. Then he revealed himself to them as well.

When Jesus appeared before the disciples, he anointed them with the Holy Spirit. His only description of such power, was to say,

"If you forgive anyone's sins, their sins are forgiven; if you do not forgive them, they are not forgiven." (33)

They were being anointed and sent to do the work of God, to serve the Father, just as Jesus had served the Father.

When we gave our lives to Christ, we too were anointed with the power of the Holy Spirit. We are being sent to become the hands and feet of God, to share the good news of the gospel with those who are unable to forgive others and themselves.

By the power of the Holy Spirit, we embody a 'nevertheless, thy will be done' lifestyle.

Prayer

Most Gracious and Heavenly Father,

Thank you for your unconditional love, mercy, and grace. May the words of our mouths and the meditations of our hearts be pleasing in your sight, Lord, our Rock and our Redeemer. (1) For all things are permissible but not everything is beneficial. Everything is permissible but not everything is edifying. (2) Therefore, seeing we also are surrounded by a great cloud of witnesses, let us lay aside every weight, and the sin which so easily besets us, and let us run with patience the race that is set before us, looking unto Jesus, the author and finisher of our faith, who for the joy that was set before Him endured the cross, despising the shame, and is set down at the right hand of the throne of God. (3)

Blessed are those who have not seen and yet have believed. (34)

In Jesus' Name,

Amen

Our Dwelling Place

Teach us to number our days, that we may gain a heart of wisdom.

Psalm 90:12

Every day that we breathe, we are in the presence of the Lord. There is nothing we have done that God is not aware of. He is our dwelling place. He is our beginning and our end. He is our creator, and we are the workmanship of his hands. God gave us creative minds to consider, ponder, develop, and be. He granted us freedom to choose right from wrong, to believe or not to believe, and to consider his way or to go our own way. However, no matter what we choose, we are in his dwelling place, an environment he created, using minds he developed, bodies he shaped, and operating with souls that are within his grasp.

Wisdom is the application of knowledge.

With every heartbeat, we are granted another opportunity to get it right. We can repent, turn to God and make him a priority in our life. Our assumption is that we will have time to make this decision. But God warns us that he will come like a thief in the night. It is our responsibility to be prepared.

When we die, God will still exist and we will still be in his dwelling place, just in a different form.

God loves us so much that he created us in his likeness. God doesn't desire to punish us for our sins. His desire is to have a relationship with us, to forgive us and for us to join together as one.

The truth is, we are finite beings with a limited time on this earth. Our bodies and this earth are limited resources created by God. We are here so that we may have the opportunity to experience life with each other, a life of creative intelligence, and a life of commitment and honor to God. As Christians, we are to point others toward God to learn more of him and the saving grace of Jesus Christ.

We know that within each man resides a spirit that is no longer present at death. We know that despite our best efforts, we will all experience pain, trouble, and sorrow. But we also will experience joy, love, and happiness. Knowledge of God grants us a peace of understanding that transcends any current situation. Knowledge of Christ transcends life on this earth and grants us access to an eternal life without pain, sorrow, or tears.

There is no person walking this earth that can grant us the peace that God provides. No person that knows us as intimately as God. No person that can define our way, map our journey, or create our destination - that right and ability belongs to God alone. God loves us. He is always for us and he desires that we win this race. But we can only get there by acknowledging that he is our dwelling place.

When we honor God with our lives, we gain favor with God and man. By the power of the Holy Spirit, we embody a 'nevertheless, thy will be done' lifestyle.

Prayer

Most Gracious and Heavenly Father,

Thank you for your unconditional love, mercy, and grace. May the words of our mouths and the meditations of our hearts be pleasing in your sight, Lord, our Rock and our Redeemer. (1) For all things are permissible but not everything is beneficial. Everything is permissible but not everything is edifying. (2) Therefore, seeing we also are surrounded by a great cloud of witnesses, let us lay aside every weight, and the sin which so easily besets us, and let us run with patience the race that is set before us, looking unto Jesus, the author and finisher of our faith, who for the joy that was set before Him endured the cross, despising the shame, and is set down at the right hand of the throne of God. (3)

Satisfy us in the morning with your unfailing love, that we may sing for joy and be glad all our days. Make us glad for as many days as you have afflicted us, for as many years as we have seen trouble. May your deeds be shown to your servants, your splendor to their children. May the favor of the Lord our God rest on us; establish the work of our hands for us—yes, establish the work of our hands. (35)

In Jesus' Name,

Amen

Honoring Our Promises to God

And Jephthah made a vow to the Lord: "If you give the Ammonites into my hands, whatever comes out of the door of my house to meet me when I return in triumph from the Ammonites will be the Lord's, and I will sacrifice it as a burnt offering."

Judges 11:30-31

When we make a vow to God, it requires that we place him first, no matter the sacrifice, even if that sacrifice is family, a good job, friends or material possessions we have worked our entire lives to achieve.

Jephthah was rejected by his brothers and refused any part of their inheritance because he was their half-brother, born of a prostitute. They shunned him and he was forced to move to a neighboring town filled with vagabonds, thieves and gang members. But Jephthah was a mighty warrior and those in great power followed his lead.

When the Israelites fell under attack, Jephthah's brothers, the sons of Gilead, came to Jephthah and begged for him to help them to defeat their enemy, the Ammonites, who were great in number.

Jephthah asked them why he should help them when they wanted nothing to do with him. They told Jephthah that he would become leader of the Gileadites. Jephthah had trouble believing them, but they swore before God they would do as they promised. Immediately, the people and elders named him head of the Gileadites.

Jephthah prayed to have victory over the Ammonites. In fact, he promised God that whatever came out of his home to greet him first, he would dedicate to the Lord in a burnt offering. God answered Jephthah's prayer and gave him a mighty victory over the Ammonites.

Upon returning home, his one and only, beautiful and unwed daughter danced in celebration of his victory. Jephthah's heart was broken and he cried out in agony, explaining to his daughter his promise to God. His daughter understood and only asked for a little time to say goodbye to her friends and mourn her inability to experience marriage. Jephthah granted her that time but did as he promised to God when she returned.

Not only did Jephthah help those who rejected him repeatedly, but he also risked the life of the one family member who loved and adored him faithfully. In gaining the one thing he'd wanted his entire life, the respect of his father's family, the Gileadites, and an inheritance from their family, he lost the one family member that he adored and who truly loved him. Those who benefited from Jephthah's sacrifice did not even understand what it cost him to provide it. They did not grasp or care how their disrespect and disconnection made Jephthah desire what he'd been deprived of since childhood (respect and justice). In the end, his leadership of the Gileadites held no true value to him but blessed them abundantly (he was indeed a man of God and a great warrior) and ultimately cost him his one true love. His loss was their gain, he blessed those who despitefully used him with the gifts of peace and security.

Jephthah made God the head of his house, the captain of his soul, and the source of his being. He believed and had faith in God, and by faith he honored God, even to the point of sacrificing his great love for a greater love. Jephthah had an intimate relationship with God, proof verified by his willingness to honor his promise to God and let go of his beloved and only child. Just as God has honored his promise to us by sacrificing his only son, Jesus Christ for our benefit, he expects us to sacrifice our best when we have made a vow to him. By the power of the Holy Spirit, we embody a 'nevertheless, thy will be done' lifestyle.

Prayer

Most Gracious and Heavenly Father,

Thank you for your unconditional love, mercy, and grace. May the words of our mouths and the meditations of our hearts be pleasing in your sight, Lord, our Rock and our Redeemer. (1) For all things are permissible but not everything is beneficial. Everything is permissible but not everything is edifying. (2) Therefore, seeing we also are surrounded by a great cloud of witnesses, let us lay aside every weight, and the sin which so easily besets us, and let us run with patience the race that is set before us, looking unto Jesus, the author and finisher of our faith, who for the joy that was set before Him endured the cross, despising the shame, and is set down at the right hand of the throne of God. (3)

You, God, are our God, earnestly we seek you; we thirst for you, our whole beings long for you, in a dry and parched land where there is no water. We have seen you in the sanctuary and beheld your power and your glory. Because your love is better than life, our lips glorify you. We will praise you as long as we live, and in your name we will lift up our hands. We will be fully satisfied as with the richest of foods; with singing lips our mouths will praise you. On our bed we remember you; we think of you through the watches of the night. Because you are our help, we sing in the shadow of your wings. We cling to you; your right hand upholds us. Those who want to kill us will be destroyed; they will go down to the depths of the earth. They will be given over to the sword and become food for jackals. But the king will rejoice in God; all who swear by God will glory in him, while the mouths of liars will be silenced. (36)

In Jesus' Name,

Amen

Pleasing to All

But thanks be to God, who always leads us as captives in Christ's triumphal procession and uses us to spread the aroma of the knowledge of him everywhere. For we are to God the pleasing aroma of Christ among those who are being saved and those who are perishing.

2 Corinthians 2:14-15

As Christians, we are to let our light shine wherever we go. We are kind, respectful, humble, forgiving and giving in all environments. In this way, we are able to share the love of Christ with those who are on their way to heaven, and those who have not yet discovered the value of God.

Our lives are full of moments. Last week, I had so many situations that could have upset me and made me behave in a way that is not kind, respectful, appreciative or understanding. But God is teaching me to let go and let him handle every issue. For every disrespectful experience, I can turn it over to him. For every upsetting day, I can lean on him. For every accident, failure, and circumstance that leads to misfortune, I can trust God to make it straight.

But the truth is, we are like batteries. We all need to rest and recharge so that we can show up and be wonderful. We all need to sit in the presence of God and allow him to download all our updates so that we can walk into every situation prepared and informed.

When we don't make rest a priority, we meet our moments and make wrong decisions. We choose to do things that are unhealthy and unholy.

When Paul writes to the church in Corinth, he opens his letter with an apology of sorts. He promises not to complain to them again because he needs to have someone that brings him joy and, in his reflections, he realized he can't make those who are his source of joy to endure his pain as well. This is a mature moment for him. He also realizes in sharing his pain, his followers have risen to defend him against the person that caused him great offense. He asks them to not only forgive that person but to also comfort them with love so that they are not hard on themselves.

Then Paul shares how wonderful, beautiful, and triumphant it is when people are in our presence. He tells us that when we are who God created us to be, people look forward to seeing us and spending time with us. They enjoy being exposed to the fruit of the Spirit and a reflection of Christ. In fact, when we are decent and in order, keeping God first and learning from him how to live a life that is truly holy and beautiful, we exceed the expectations of those around us to the point they feel they must give God glory!

When God's will becomes our will, we become a perfect conduit of Christ's message and his love. By the power of the Holy Spirit, we embody a 'nevertheless, thy will be done' lifestyle.

Prayer

Most Gracious and Heavenly Father,

Thank you for your unconditional love, mercy, and grace. May the words of our mouths and the meditations of our hearts be pleasing in your sight, Lord, our Rock and our Redeemer. (1) For all things are permissible but not everything is beneficial. Everything is permissible but not everything is edifying. (2) Therefore, seeing we also are surrounded by a great cloud of witnesses, let us lay aside every weight, and the sin which so easily besets us, and let us run with patience the race that is set before us, looking unto Jesus, the author and finisher of our faith, who for the joy that was set before Him endured the cross, despising the shame, and is set down at the right hand of the throne of God. (3)

Lord, help us to share the love of Christ with everyone we encounter. Love is patient, love is kind. It does not envy, it does not boast, it is not proud. It does not dishonor others, it is not self-seeking, it is not easily angered, it keeps no record of wrongs. (37)

In Jesus' Name,

Amen

Pencil-Thin Victories

The Lord said to Joshua, "Stand up!
What are you doing down on your face?"

Joshua 7:10

When we are walking with God, we can feel impenetrable. We may have walked with excellence for so long, we expect to receive honor and victory everywhere that we go. But we can take these moments for granted and assume that our decisions are always healthy and right. But God sees all and knows all. He will judge in fairness and his decisions are final.

Joshua became a leader to the Israelites after Moses passed away. He'd just led them in a miraculous victory against Jericho, where they defeated a well-known fortified city. Joshua sent men to spy out the city of Ai. The men came back with a good report and shared that Joshua could send a fraction of their men and defeat the city. Instead, Joshua's army was defeated in the battle, and this made all their hearts drop with fear and trembling at what could be next.

As Joshua and the elders of Israel fell in sackcloth, prayer and seeking understanding before God, God told Joshua that their defeat was connected to someone who has taken something that does not belong to them and lied to cover their action which caused their defeat. God told him to identify who it was and to remove them from their camp, immediately.

Joshua did as instructed. Once complete, God told

Joshua,

"Do not be afraid; do not be discouraged. Take the whole army with you, and go up and attack Ai. For I have delivered into your hands the king of Ai, his people, his city and his land. You shall do to Ai and its king as you did to Jericho and its king, except that you may carry off their plunder and livestock for yourselves. Set an ambush behind the city." (38)

God then told them exactly what to do and insisted they follow his instruction implicitly. They did exactly as God instructed and were granted the victory.

Our victories are tied to our obedience and honor of God and his will. God gave us the ten commandments as a hedge of protection. He gave us the beatitudes to serve as a lantern in the darkness. He sent us the Holy Spirit to comfort, remind, and convict us when necessary. Our battles can't be won if we aren't walking according to the will of God. Our victorious lives can be shattered if we aren't careful. Pencil-thin victories are those which God has been gracious enough to shine a light on our dark places and has given us the mercy to course correct so that we can obtain the victory. Today we must choose his will over ours. In doing so, God will give us unique strategies by which to outsmart our enemy and win. By the power of the Holy Spirit, we embody a 'nevertheless, thy will be done' lifestyle.

Prayer

Most Gracious and Heavenly Father,

Thank you for your unconditional love, mercy, and grace. May the words of our mouths and the meditations of our hearts be pleasing in your sight, Lord, our Rock and our Redeemer. (1) For all things are permissible but not everything is beneficial. Everything is permissible but not everything is edifying. (2) Therefore, seeing we also are surrounded by a great cloud of witnesses, let us lay aside every weight, and the sin which so easily besets us, and let us run with patience the race that is set before us, looking unto Jesus, the author and finisher of our faith, who for the joy that was set before Him endured the cross, despising the shame, and is set down at the right hand of the throne of God. (3)

SPEECHLESS

Why do the nations conspire and the people plot in vain? The kings of the earth rise up and the rulers band together against the Lord and against his anointed, saying, "Let us break their chains and throw off their shackles." The One enthroned in heaven laughs; the Lord scoffs at them. He rebukes them in his anger and terrifies them in his wrath, saying, "I have installed my king on Zion, my holy mountain." I will proclaim the Lord's decree: He said to us, "You are my sons; today I have become your father. Ask me, and I will make the nations your inheritance, the ends of the earth your possession. You will break them with a rod of iron; you will dash them to pieces like pottery." Therefore, you kings, be wise; be warned, you rulers of the earth. Serve the Lord with fear and celebrate his rule with trembling. Kiss his son, or he will be angry and your way will lead to your destruction, for his wrath can flare up in a moment. Blessed are all who take refuge in him. (39)

In Jesus' Name,

Amen

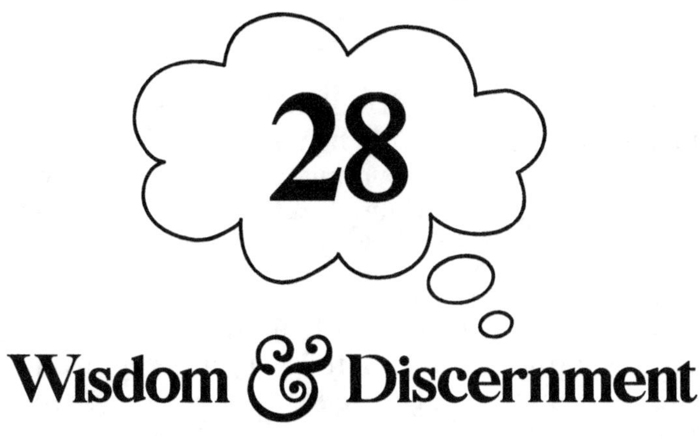

28

Wisdom & Discernment

He sent them to Bethlehem and said, "Go and search carefully for the child. As soon as you find him, report to me, so that I too may go and worship him."

Matthew 2:8

Recognizing intention is a skill that is led by intuition but is often supported by the facets of wisdom, discernment, and revelation. We must learn to acknowledge and respond to our intuition, without considering the threat of consequence, especially when the stakes are high.

When men of ancient Persia (now Iran) arrived in Jerusalem seeking the new born king of the Jews, whispers of their presence and purpose reached King Herod. Herod felt a certain threat to his kingdom and immediately summoned Jewish leadership to share the location of the child. Then he secretly summoned the Magi (ancient wise men of Persia) to inquire of when the child was born. Herod also asked the Magi to return and share the exact location of the child so that he too could worship. The Magi agreed to do so.

As the Magi arrived in Bethlehem, they were led by a star in the sky to Jesus. They bowed before the Lord in worship bearing gifts. It was also at this time that they received a revelation that King Herod's intentions were felonious and were advised not to return to him with the location of Jesus. Rather than return to King Herod, the wise men went home, satisfied that they met their responsibility of honoring the new born king of the Jews.

Soon after, Herod realized the Magi were not going to return with the information he'd requested. So, Herod created a law that stated all young boys under the age of two in Bethlehem were to be killed. But God had already revealed in a dream to Mary and Joseph to take Jesus to Egypt, where he would be safe.

When someone brings a gift, it often signifies honor, respect, and adoration. But a gift is very different from worship, an indication of reverence, authority, and trust. The Magi traveled a great distance to honor Jesus with their worship, but also brought him the gifts of gold, frankincense, and myrrh. Finally, they honored his life by defying the king of the land, a person of great authority and ability, to save the life of the one who would eventually offer salvation to us all.

Our lives are full of complexity, adventure, and wonder. The experiences we share are determined by our passion, responsibility, and curiosity of life. Somewhere along our life paths we begin to discover who we are and how we can best serve the world around us. We determine how we hope others will perceive us but more importantly, who we are at the core of our being. It is in these moments, when we recognize ill intent toward others, that we decide to take a different course, and go the way God instructs. By the power of the Holy Spirit, we embody a 'nevertheless, thy will be done' lifestyle.

Prayer

Most Gracious and Heavenly Father,

Thank you for your unconditional love, mercy, and grace. May the words of our mouths and the meditations of our hearts be pleasing in your sight, Lord, our Rock and our Redeemer. (1) For all things are permissible but not everything is beneficial. Everything is permissible but not everything is edifying. (2) Therefore, seeing we also are surrounded by a great cloud of witnesses, let us lay aside every weight, and the sin which so easily besets us, and let us run with patience the race that is set before us, looking unto Jesus, the author and finisher of our faith, who for the joy that was set before Him endured the cross, despising the shame, and is set down at the right hand of the throne of

God. (3)

Let us be wise to listen and add to our learning, and let us be discerning to get guidance—for understanding proverbs and parables, the sayings and riddles of the wise. The fear of the Lord is the beginning of knowledge, but fools despise wisdom and instruction. (40)

In Jesus' Name,

Amen

Giving God Our Best

Then the Lord said to Cain, "Why are you angry? Why is your face downcast? If you do what is right, will you not be accepted? But if you do not do what is right, sin is crouching at your door; it desires to have you, but you must rule over it."

Genesis 4:6-7

Failing to do our best can lead to sin. When we see others gaining what we desire because of their discipline, hard-work, and commitment we can make decisions that are even more destructive than the bad choices that brought us to our current position.

Discipline requires that we show up and do what must be done whether we desire to do so or not. It is what ensures we give God the first of our day, the first of our tithe, the first of our praise, and the first of our fruit. Discipline is the core behind developing systems that create consistent results.

Hard-work is the difference between doing your best and doing enough to get by. When we show up and give one hundred percent, leaving nothing on the floor (as they say), we are making sure that we have done all that we can do to ensure the best outcome. Behind the principle of hard work is responsibility. It is our responsibility to stop and correct what we can when we see that something is wrong.

Commitment says yes and shows up to do what was promised. Commitment takes our good intentions and develops them into good works. Commitment holds us accountable.

When we do our best, we are giving that to God as a thank you for the abilities, opportunities, and outcomes he grants in our lives. When Cain realized that he could do better but chose not to, God gave him a clear warning. He warned him that not doing our best makes sin look more appealing. Mediocrity gives us an excuse to fall, fail, and make felonious decisions. Cain murdered his brother out of jealousy and self-loathing. But in doing so, he also subjected himself to a life of reflection, by disabling himself to do what God created him to do.

When we are intentional about our worship, God protects us from such outcomes. He takes the time to guide us in the way we should go. He protects us from harm and danger. Even though Cain sinned, God protected him with a mark and promised to avenge anyone that dared to hurt him. Despite Cain's mediocrity, he worshiped God and had a relationship with God, and God continued to protect him.

We are blessed to give God our best. By the power of the Holy Spirit, we embody a 'nevertheless, thy will be done' lifestyle.

Prayer

Most Gracious and Heavenly Father,

Thank you for your unconditional love, mercy, and grace. May the words of our mouths and the meditations of our hearts be pleasing in your sight, Lord, our Rock and our Redeemer. (1) For all things are permissible but not everything is beneficial. Everything is permissible but not everything is edifying. (2) Therefore, seeing we also are surrounded by a great cloud of witnesses, let us lay aside every weight, and the sin which so easily besets us, and let us run with patience the race that is set before us, looking unto Jesus, the author and finisher of our faith, who for the joy that was set before Him endured the cross, despising the shame, and is set down at the right hand of the throne of God. (3)

We flee youthful passions and pursue righteousness, faith, love, and peace, along with those who call on the Lord from a pure heart. We have nothing to do with foolish, ignorant controversies; for they breed quarrels. As the Lord's servant, we must not be quarrelsome but kind to everyone, able to teach, patiently enduring evil, correcting our opponents with gentleness. Perhaps God may grant them repentance leading to a knowledge of the truth, and they may come to their senses and escape from the snare of the devil, after being captured by him to do his will. (40)

In Jesus' Name,

Amen

Let Our Actions Say So

But someone will say, "You have faith; I have deeds." Show me your faith without deeds, and I will show you my faith by my deeds.

James 2:18

Our behaviors are directly connected to what we believe. When we say one thing but take an action in contradiction, we are openly declaring what we believe in our hearts by the path we take. When we plant seeds of hope within our souls, it is our responsibility to water that seed by taking the appropriate steps to see it come to pass. If we desire something, as God directs us, we should seek it strategically, in thought, word, and deed.

As ambassadors of Christ, our first hope and belief should be to please him in all that we say and do. We are to respect, love, forgive, protect, and give to others. Our righteousness is connected to what we do… it is not simply what we believe for we reflect what we believe by what we do. When we tithe, keep God first, love our neighbors as ourselves, and go above and beyond to worship God by praying, seeking him, and meditating on his word, day and night - we juxtapose our actions against our words, giving life. It is as though our thoughts show up in black and white, but our actions are in color.

Rather than imagine what life could be, let's live the life we hope to have. Let's treat everyone with respect and honor. Let's forgive others as we will and have sought forgiveness many times and received it. When we show mercy, we are extending love. Let's give often and without concern for God loves a cheerful giver! Our generosity toward others is also a gift. Whether we are providing a helping hand or simply giving someone something nice, it feels good and reflects the love of God when we give. Let's pay attention to others so that we may nurture and protect them when it is in our ability to do so.

Faith without works is dead. Let our actions line up with what we imagine in our hearts. Love is a noun, but it is more importantly, a verb. As God has been faithful to give us love, it is our responsibility to pay it forward. By the power of the Holy Spirit, we embody a 'nevertheless, thy will be done' lifestyle.

Prayer

Most Gracious and Heavenly Father,

Thank you for your unconditional love, mercy, and grace. May the words of our mouths and the meditations of our hearts be pleasing in your sight, Lord, our Rock and our Redeemer. (1) For all things are permissible but not everything is beneficial. Everything is permissible but not everything is edifying. (2) Therefore, seeing we also are surrounded by a great cloud of witnesses, let us lay aside every weight, and the sin which so easily besets us, and let us run with patience the race that is set before us, looking unto Jesus, the author and finisher of our faith, who for the joy that was set before Him endured the cross, despising the shame, and is set down at the right hand of the throne of God. (3)

We rejoice in the Lord always. We allow our gentleness to be evident to all for the Lord is near. We are not anxious about anything, but in every situation, by prayer and petition, with thanksgiving, we present our requests to God. And the peace of God, which transcends all understanding, will guard our hearts and our minds in Christ Jesus. Whatever is true, whatever is noble, whatever is right, whatever is pure, whatever is lovely, whatever is admirable—if anything is excellent or praiseworthy—we think about such things. Whatever we have learned or received or heard from our Christian leaders—we put it into practice. And the God of peace will be with us. (41)

In Jesus' Name,

Amen

Never the Less

"Father, if you are willing, take this cup from me; yet not my will, but yours be done." An angel from heaven appeared to him and strengthened him. And being in anguish, he prayed more earnestly, and his sweat was like drops of blood falling to the ground.

Luke 22:42-44

Sometimes when we are walking in obedience to the will of God, we are met with a request for extreme sacrifice. We have witnessed such willingness in Abraham, who was willing to sacrifice a son he'd dreamt of having his entire life; in three Hebrew boys sentenced to death in a fiery furnace; Daniel in the lion's den; and Stephen stoned before the religious leaders. This level of obedience is not intended for the faint of heart, but for those who are completely and totally dependent on God. This is a true test of faith, one that even Jesus himself found difficult.

As Jesus prepared for his last supper with his disciples, in honor of the Passover, one of his disciples offered to betray Jesus for a price. Judas, one of the Lord's twelve disciples, promised the enemy of Christ that he would help them to capture him and that they may subsequently kill him.

During the supper, Jesus told the disciples what to expect in the time to come. They were saddened and curious about what the future would bring. Jesus also explained that the person that would betray him sat there among them. While they pondered this, they also wondered who among them was the greatest. Jesus shared that the best among them would not only lead but would also serve.

Then Jesus and his disciples went to the Mount of Olives to pray. Jesus separated from the men and prayed to God about his assignment and the upcoming season. His life was in God's hands and he had to let go. His strength left his body as he prayed, and he was so nervous he sweat to the point of bleeding. But an angel of the Lord strengthened him to continue.

When he finished praying, he was captured by the religious leaders, led by his disciple, Judas. There was a great commotion as one of his disciples attempted to protect him from the enemy by wielding a sword. But Jesus, who was committed to the will of God put it to an end and went willingly with the men, stating it was the hour for darkness to reign.

In our lives, God will ask us to make sacrifices that are painful. This is a test of our faith. No matter the perceived outcome, we must be willing to take the route God has assigned. Even if it feels as though darkness has been permitted to reign in our situation. We must trust God. By the power of the Holy Spirit, we embody a 'nevertheless, thy will be done' lifestyle.

Prayer

Most Gracious and Heavenly Father,

Thank you for your unconditional love, mercy, and grace. May the words of our mouths and the meditations of our hearts be pleasing in your sight, Lord, our Rock and our Redeemer. (1) For all things are permissible but not everything is beneficial. Everything is permissible but not everything is edifying. (2) Therefore, seeing we also are surrounded by a great cloud of witnesses, let us lay aside every weight, and the sin which so easily besets us, and let us run with patience the race that is set before us, looking unto Jesus, the author and finisher of our faith, who for the joy that was set before Him endured the cross, despising the shame, and is set down at the right hand of the throne of God. (3)

The enemies of Christ will seize us and persecute us. They will hand us over to synagogues and put us in prison, and we will be brought before kings and governors, and all on account of the name of Jesus. And we will bear the testimony of Christ. But we have made up our mind not to worry beforehand how we will defend ourselves. For you will give us words and wisdom that none of our adversaries will be able to resist or contradict. We will be betrayed even by parents, brothers and sisters, relatives and friends, and they will put some of us to death. Everyone will hate us because of Christ. But not a hair of our head will perish. We will stand firm, and we will win life. (42)

Satan has asked to sift us as wheat. But Christ has prayed for us, that our faith may not fail. And when we have turned back, we must strengthen our brothers. (43)

In Jesus Name,

Amen

Citations

1. Psalm 19:14
2. 1 Corinthians 10:23
3. Hebrews 12:1-2
4. Colossians 3:17
5. Ezekiel 37:12 -14
6. Jonah 2:2-9
7. Psalm 40:4-8
8. Psalm 121
9. Psalm 19:7-14
10. Psalm 124
11. Psalm 139
12. I Samuel 15:22b
13. Psalm 40:6-17
14. Daniel 6:6-8
15. Daniel 6:16
16. Daniel 6:26b
17. Luke 6:27-36
18. Philippians 1:9-11
19. Ephesians 6:11-20
20. Psalm 145:9-21
21. Hebrews 12:1-3
22. Philippians 2:1-5

23. Psalm 23
24. Matthew 5:16
25. 2 Corinthians 8:5
26. Mark 8:35-38
27. Psalm 51:10-19
28. Ephesians 4:1-7
29. Matthew 6:9-13
30. Psalm 27:11-14
31. Numbers 23:19
32. Psalm 139:14-18
33. John 20:23
34. John 20:29
35. Psalm 90:14-17
36. Psalm 63
37. I Corinthians 13:4-5
38. Joshua 8:1-2
39. Psalm 2
40. Proverbs 1:5-7
40b. 2 Timothy 2:22-26
41. Philippians 4: 4-8
42. Luke 21:12-19
43. Luke 22:31-32

About the Author

At the age of 9, Stephanie was molested by a friend of my family. In high school, she held the hand of a friend as he died from a fatal gun shot wound... As an adult, she was the victim of a violent acquaintance rape. Subsequently, she struggled with personal demons. But when she sought the Lord and his Word, her life was forever changed.

Give God ALL the Glory!

He is and will always be the head of my life. He is my joy, my strength, my everything.
My constant prayer is to be a perfect conduit of his message and love.

Stephanie was born in Muskogee, Oklahoma. She graduated from Putnam City North High School in 1994. She was married for 16 years. She is the mother of 3 beautiful daughters, and has a grandson named Levi. She graduated with her Associates in Technology, a Bachelor of Arts in Communications, and a Master of Arts in Communication with an emphasis in Political Communication.

She holds several design and technology certifications and has won numerous awards in that area. Stephanie has worked in television, print and web media for more than 16 years.

She is the owner of Moore Marketing and Communications. Her company offers strategic marketing and communication plans, media purchases, public relations, writing services, print services, graphic design and web design. Stephanie has also served as a poltical consultant for Governor, Lt. Governor, State Representative, Mayoral and City Council candidates.

Stephanie has created and sponsored teen etiquette and leadership programs for young ladies and young men. The program for young ladies is called, She's a BOSSE (A Beautiful Oasis of Success, Style and Elegance) and the young man's program is called Grindaholix: Young Men on the Rise.

To date, Stephanie has authored 25 books, 16 of which are daily devotionals. To learn more, visit mooretoread.com.

ECHOES

31 Day Devotional
HIS
favor
stephanie d.
It's not about obtaining HIS favor...
It's about recognizing you already have it!

The Living Proof!
A 31-DAY DEVOTIONAL
ON THE POWER OF YOUR WORDS
by stephanie d.

NOTHING IS BIGGER THAN OUR GOD!
OBEY
obedience breaks every yoke
by stephanie d. moore
31 Day Devotional Divine Leadership

31-Day Devotional
INTO THE
Promised Land
stephanie d. moore
Desperately Seeking the Presence of God
in the Wilderness on Your Journey
INTO THE PROMISED LAND!

BETRAYED
FAMILY SECRETS
by stephanie d. moore

31 DAY DEVOTIONAL
And God is able to make all grace abound to you, so that always having all sufficiency in everything, you may have an abundance for every good deed
2 Corinthians 9:8
ABUNDANCE
Faith & Wisdom
MOVING YOUR MOUNTAIN
by stephanie d. moore

blush
you are the apple of my eye
A 31-DAY DEVOTIONAL
OF GOD'S UNENDING LOVE FOR YOU
stephanie d. moore

I AM
DELIVERED!
by stephanie d. moore
HIS GRACE
HIS STRENGTH

www.ingramcontent.com/pod-product-compliance
Lightning Source LLC
LaVergne TN
LVHW010933110826
845149LV00013B/2575

* 9 7 8 1 9 5 5 5 4 4 4 4 3 *